A Workman That Needeth

Not to Be Ashamed

by

Frank Bateman Stanger

First Fruits Press
Wilmore, Kentucky
c2012

asburyseminary.edu
800.2ASBURY
204 North Lexington Avenue
Wilmore, Kentucky 40390

First Fruits
THE ACADEMIC OPEN PRESS OF ASBURY SEMINARY

ISBN: 9780914368922

A Workman That Needeth Not to Be Ashamed, by Frank Bateman Stanger.
First Fruits Press, © 2012
Pentecostal Publishing Company, © 1958

Digital version at
http://place.asburyseminary.edu/firstfruitsheritagematerial/10/

Stanger, Frank Bateman.
    A workman that needeth not to be ashamed / by Frank Bateman Stanger.
    Wilmore, Ky. : First Fruits Press, c2012.
    Reprint. Previously published: Louisville, Ky. : Pentecostal Publishing
    Company, c1958.
    228 p. : ill. ; 21 cm. – (Freitas lectures ; 1956)
    ISBN: 9780914368922 (pbk.)
    1. Theology, Practical. 2. Preaching. I. Title. II. Asbury Theological
    Seminary. Freitas lectures ; 1956.
    BV3 .S8 2012

Cover design by Haley Hill

asburyseminary.edu
800.2ASBURY
204 North Lexington Avenue
Wilmore, Kentucky 40390

First Fruits
THE ACADEMIC OPEN PRESS OF ASBURY SEMINARY

A WORKMAN THAT
NEEDETH NOT TO BE ASHAMED

These chapters comprise the Freitas Lectures given by the author at Asbury Theological Seminary, Wilmore, Kentucky, during the fall of 1956. Building upon the exhortation of the Apostle Paul to Timothy, his "son" in the Christian ministry —"Study to show thyself approved unto God, a workman that needeth not to be ashamed" (II Timothy 2:15)—the author speaks out of his own experience as a pastor to those who are ministers or who are preparing themselves for the Christian ministry.

It is the author's conviction that in an age when society, in general, with its galaxy of problems and its multiplicity of needs demands skillful leaders and skilled workers, even more does the Christian Society require at its head and at its heart "workmen that need not to be ashamed." An irreverent, self-seeking society has caused the church to answer for enough indictments; let not the church itself add to this list by failing to provide for itself capable and consecrated "workmen." The contemporary age demands the church at its best. If the church is to be at its best, then those who lead and serve it must be "workmen who need not to be ashamed."

The aim of the book is utterly pragmatic. The author endeavors to point out some of the practical methods by which a minister may be "a workman that needeth not to be ashamed." After an opening chapter on "The Distinctiveness of the Minister's Task," the author proceeds to discuss such practical matters as the minister's care of the church, the continuing preparations of the minister, the minister's spiritual leadership of his people, the minister and Healing, and the minister in his relationship to the world.

*A WORKMAN THAT NEEDETH NOT
TO BE ASHAMED*

A Workman That Needeth
Not to Be Ashamed

- By -

FRANK BATEMAN STANGER

THE HERALD PRESS
(*Pentecostal Publishing Co.*)
LOUISVILLE, KENTUCKY

Set up and printed by THE HERALD
PRESS, Louisville, Kentucky

FOREWORD

The contents of this book were given as The Freitas Lectures at Asbury Theological Seminary, Wilmore, Kentucky, in November 1956. The George and Elizabeth Freitas Lectureship has been established by Mrs. Elizabeth Freitas of Modesto, California, as a memorial to her husband, George Freitas, and as an expression of her interest in the training of a ministry on the highest level in spiritual attainment and practical achievement. Each year The Freitas Lectures are given in the field of Applied Theology at Asbury Theological Seminary.

The author is grateful to President Julian C. McPheeters, to Dean W. D. Turkington, and to the honored members of the faculty of Asbury Theological Seminary both for the invitation to deliver The Freitas Lectures and for the innumerable courtesies and kindnesses extended him at the time the lectures were given.

The author is likewise grateful to his secretary, Miss Velma L. Quinn, for her typing of the original lectures; and to Mrs. Shirley Latch for her typing of the revised manuscript in preparation for publication.

DEDICATED
with love
to my wife
MARDELLE
who as
"a workman that needeth not to be ashamed"
in our parsonage and church life
has constantly inspired me to be
"a workman that needeth not to be ashamed"
in my Christian ministry.

ACKNOWLEDGMENTS

The author is grateful to the following publishers for their very kind permission to quote from the books enumerated:

ABINGDON PRESS: E. S. Jones, *Abundant Living;* E. S. Jones, *The Christ of the Indian Road;* E. S. Jones, *Growing Spiritually;* W. E. Sangster, *Let Me Commend;* W. E. Sangster, *The Pure in Heart;* L. D. Weatherhead, *Psychology, Religion, and Healing.*

THE CHRISTIAN CENTURY FOUNDATION: selected poems and selections from the writings of Simeon Stylites

JOHN DAY CO.: L. Yutang, *My Country and My People*

DIAL PRESS: G. Schmitt, *David the King*

DOUBLEDAY & CO.: J. Street, *The Gauntlet*

HARPER & BROTHERS: A. E. Day, *An Autobiography of Prayer;* W. J. Hyde, *Dig or Die, Brother Hyde;* E. Trueblood, *Signs of Hope*

ARTHUR JAMES, LTD.: E. H. Salmon, *He Heals Today*

THE MACMILLAN CO.: R. T. Coffin, *Yankee Coast;* J. B. Phillips, *Letters to Young Churches*

NEW YORK TIMES MAGAZINE: quotations from an article by Arnold Toynbee

FLEMING H. REVELL CO.: P. Marshall, *Mr. Jones, Meet the Master*

PRINCETON UNIVERSITY PRESS: P. E. More,
Pages from an Oxford Diary

THE ROTARIAN: miscellaneous quotations

CHARLES SCRIBNERS SONS: C. A. Lindbergh,
The Spirit of St. Louis

SIMON & SCHUSTER: H. M. Robinson, *The Cardinal*

TIME MAGAZINE: book review of *Dear Charles* by
W. Shader

WOMAN'S DIVISION OF CHRISTIAN SERVICE,
THE METHODIST CHURCH: F. G. Ensley, *Paul's
Letters to Local Churches*

THE WESTMINSTER PRESS: D. A. MacLennon,
Entrusted with the Gospel

Sincere gratitude is, likewise, expressed to the
author's friend, Dr. W. E. Sangster, for kind permission to quote from his pamphlets "A Spiritual Check-Up" and a "Check-Up for Our Church."

CONTENTS

FOREWORD

ACKNOWLEDGMENTS (Page)

Chapter I
A Workman That Needeth Not to Be Ashamed 13

Chapter II   Not Ashamed
—Because of the Distinctiveness of His Task 23

Chapter III Not Ashamed
—In His Continuing Preparations 49

Chapter IV   Not Ashamed
—In His Care of the Church 93

Chapter V   Not Ashamed
—In His Spiritual Leadership of His people 125

Chapter VI   Not Ashamed
—In His Ministry of Healing 155

Chapter VII Not Ashamed
—In His Relation to the World 188

CONCLUSION

CHAPTER I

THE MINISTER—A WORKMAN THAT NEEDETH NOT TO BE ASHAMED

"Study to show thyself approved unto God, a workman that needeth not to be ashamed . . . "
II Timothy 2:15

In conformity to the avowed purpose of this Lectureship I have been asked to speak these days within the field of Practical Theology. Generally speaking, Practical Theology means the application of the moral and spiritual insights gained by theological study to the needs of persons and to the requirements of satisfactory human relationships. In particular we can say that Practical Theology means the Church of Christ at work. Especially does Practical Theology refer to the Christian Church at the local level; that is, to the local unit of a denomination, the parish church—the church at the country crossroads, or the church at the heart of the city, or the church along Desirable Avenue in the suburbs, or the church on the college campus, or the church in the lovely village, or the church in the migrant settlement.

Speaking personally, I am delighted that I was asked to lecture within the area of Practical Theology. The local church, the church responsible for a definite parish, has been my life. Twenty-two years ago my annual conference entrusted me with my first parish assignment.

I often think back over the path that I have journeyed through local church after local church, and my thoughts, passing through the stage of memories that "bless and burn," suddenly are changed into prayers—prayers to Almighty God who "counted me worthy to be called into the ministry of His dear Son," prayers of thanksgiving for the privileges that have been mine along the way, prayers of gratitude for all that my parish pilgrimages have taught me about the work of the local church in particular and the task of the Christian ministry in general.

May I be permitted to reminisce a little in order to illustrate something of what I mean? My first pastoral assignment was a two-point circuit. One church consisted of a handful of Methodists, a half dozen of families, in the midst of an overwhelmingly predominant Roman Catholic community. Perhaps the only lesson I learned here was the fact that God's love in human hearts, made real by the Cross of Jesus Christ, creates a love for the church, and a faithfulness to the church, that are undying. The other church on my first circuit was a crossroads charge, characterized by a small Official Board, in which the authority of men and of women was about evenly matched. It was here that I began to discover that the minister must beware of becoming a mere "puppet" in the hands of those who are accustomed to "running the show."

I then moved to another country charge, where I learned early one of the most valuable lessons of my ministry. As minister I became the "victim" of a church faction. In the midst of it all I learned how wonderfully Christian some folk are spiritually capable of remaining, even under the bitterest circumstances, and on the other hand, I saw to what "devilish levels" unregenerate folk within a church can sink when suddenly provoked. It was then that I learned that the only safe ideal for a church's life is Christ—Christ is the object of the Church, Christ is the pattern of the Church, Christ is the spirit of the Church, Christ is the life of the Church!

It was in this same church that I had the unique experience of being present at a Board meeting when it was suggested that my salary be lowered. A member of the Board had suggested that, in view of my educational attainments, my salary should be raised two hundred dollars. Immediately one of the factious brethren declared, "If you ask me, I think the pastor's salary ought to be lowered one hundred dollars. That's just the trouble with the world today—too much education." Oh, well, such is life—a pastor's life!

My Annual Conference then sent me to a village, where for the first time I "got the feel" of being the leader of a church. Then on to a borough, where my ministerial leadership was not only welcomed and appreciated, but where it was also rewarded by visible results both spiritual and material.

Perhaps the greatest opportunity of my ministry, certainly up to that time, was my being sent to a challenging church in a lovely suburban borough, a situation concerning which my beloved District Superintendent had said to me, "You will be doing wrong if you do not go." Here was a suburban church with a superb opportunity! What a happy ministry I had there, and seemingly there were commendable results to show for it. It was there that my philosophy of the pastoral ministry became crystallized and that my techniques of church administration began to assume the pattern of proved formulae.

The church that I serve now is a wonderful church with a great spiritual tradition—revivals, evangelism, emphasis upon the Deeper Life, interest in missions, young people going out into full-time Christian service. The great challenge here has been to conserve the values of the past and make them contributory to aggressive activity and to progressive accomplishment. The light must never go out, the salt must never lose its savor, the city must always maintain its hill-top location!

In our day I believe that we are witnessing a new emphasis upon the significance and importance of the place of the local church in the total work of the Christian church. Certainly this is illustrated by the words and actions of two distinguished Methodist pastors, serving downtown churches in the nation's two largest cities, who might easily have been elected to the Methodist episcopacy in recent years if they had permitted their names to remain in the voting.

For many years, said Rev. Ralph W. Sockman of Christ Church, New York City, I have been convinced that the greatest need of the contemporary church is the strengthening of the local pulpit. There is a tragic lag between the pronouncements of general church conventions and the practices of local church congregations. We can never exalt the pulpit properly as long as we regard it as a steppingstone to administrative positions. Having held and taught these convictions, I would now seem inconsistent in leaving the pulpit for the bishopric.

Rev. Charles R. Goff of the Chicago Temple said that he had some misgivings as he allowed his name to appear on four ballots. He remembered that he had resisted the call to the Temple, and he had been wrong. The ministry there had been a great experience, he said, and he sees no reason why it should lose interest.

"I went there 10 years ago without much knowledge of the city. I was a country boy, and I still am. I found out a few things in 10 years, and I don't think that ought to be wasted."

And the editor who recorded the above statements added significantly:

In these days when we need great preaching so desperately, the pulpit towers far above the administrative (or editorial) desk. The pastor's contacts with the people in the pews, with personal needs, and enthusiasms, and blind spots, are vastly more important than any knowledge of over-all plans and programs. The best applications of the social aspects of the gospel start with the use of the personal gospel in the home church, and work for the world-wide church begins not in some faraway conference but in the home community. (The Christian Advocate)

Or take the contemporary case of the Rev. David A. MacLennan, famed minister of Timothy Eaton Memorial Church, Toronto, Canada, who was called to a Professorship of Homiletics in the Yale Divinity School, and who has chosen to return to the pastorate of a church. His article entitled "Why I Returned to the Parish Ministry ("United Church Observer", December 15, 1955) is most significant. Among other things he writes:

> Despite "security of tenure" (which could be terminated only by what is charitably and vaguely described as an "act of moral turpitude"), four months' vacation from classes each year, and the prestige of a professorship in the Ivy League, I deliberately and enthusiastically accepted the invitation to return to the front line of the parish ministry. Why? Because of the inescapable conviction that for this kind of ministry I was called, as for this vocation I had been trained. Baffling or quixotic as it may seem to those on the outside, every minister knows what Paul meant when he cried, "Woe is me if I preach not the gospel." Can you not preach it from a professorial chair? Assuredly. Nevertheless, to be one of our blessed Lord's undershepherds of a continuing, even if constantly changing flock, I regard as the most wonderful service open to any man.
>
> Other reasons derive from this one. To be Christianly involved in the lives of both sexes and all ages, to know them in their family life, to share in the inclusive programme of the living Church so that the body of Christ may be the conscience and the consolation, the spiritual home for all sorts and conditions of men, provides more durable satisfactions than any situation I know.

A world-known administrative leader of one of our major denominations once said to me in a private conversation, "I would give anything to be back in the pastorate.

Thus, if the local parish church is so important, it becomes imperative that the local church be served by efficient and effective "workmen." The minister must be "a workman that needeth not to be ashamed." The Apostle Paul, the greatest of all "spiritual workmen" in the Early Church, in writing to his beloved "son" in the ministry, exhorts him in these words: "Study to show thyself approved unto God, a workman that needeth not to be ashamed, rightly dividing the word of truth." (II Timothy 2:15)

It is characteristic of the Pauline ideal and spirit that he writes to Timothy about being a workman who is not ashamed. Paul was not ashamed of the Gospel of Christ, for he declares it to be the power of God unto salvation to every one who believes. (Romans 1:16.) Writing to the Romans the Apostle reminds them that whoever believes on Christ shall not be ashamed. (9:33; 10:11.) Likewise, Christian "hope maketh not ashamed." (Romans 5:5.) Paul desired that his life should be so exemplary that in nothing he would be ashamed. (Philippians 1:20.) Nor was the Apostle ashamed of the authority behind his ministry: "for though I should boast somewhat more of our authority, which the Lord hath given us for edification, and not for your destruction, I should not be ashamed." (II Corinthians 10:8.) And the Apostle's confidence in the One he served caused him to be free from any kind of shame, even in the midst of sufferings, which to many would have appeared as occasions of derision. He boldly declares: "For the which cause I also suffer these things: nevertheless I am not ashamed: for I know whom I have believed, and am persuaded that He is able to keep that which I have committed unto Him against that day." (II Timothy 1:12.) Little wonder is it then that in another place he reminds Timothy not to be ashamed of the testimony of our Lord. (II Timothy 1:8.)

And so to St. Paul the spirit of life and the quality

of the workmanship of the Christian Ministry must be that of "a workman that needeth not to be ashamed." By his very life and work the minister is to "make full proof" of his ministry. (II Timothy 4:5.) The Apostle, after describing for Titus the characteristics of a faithful minister of the Gospel, warns that "he that is of the contrary part" is the one to be ashamed. (Titus 2:8.) Hence, the Christian minister is to conduct himself and to serve his Lord in such a manner that "he shall be a vessel unto honor, sanctified, and meet for the Master's use, and prepared unto every good work. (II Timothy 2:21.)

In an age when society, in general, with its galaxy of problems and its multiplicity of needs demands skillful leaders and skilled workers, even more does the Christian society require at its head and at its heart "workmen that need not to be ashamed." An irreverent, self-seeking society has caused the church to answer for enough indictments; let not the church itself add to this list by failing to provide for itself capable and consecrated "workmen." The contemporary age demands the church at its best. If the church is to be at its best, then those who lead and serve it must be "workmen who need not to be ashamed." How imperative in our day is the Pauline ideal of the Christian ministry: "giving no offence in anything, that the ministry be not blamed; but in all things approving ourselves as the ministers of God . . ."(II Corinthians 6:3, 4.)

During these hours together in this series of lectures, we shall endeavor to study some of the *practical* methods by which a minister may become "a workman that needeth not to be ashamed." My method of procedure might be classified as "personal pragmatism," if the philosophy department will permit such a coined term. Perhaps it will be too personal, if not too pragmatic. Believe me when I say that I have not perused a single volume on the life and work of the Christian minister in specific and direct preparation for this series of lectures. Rather, I have chosen to speak altogether out of my own life and ministry.

I propose to discuss the general theme "A Workman That Needeth Not to be Ashamed" under the following headings:

"Not Ashamed—Because of the Distinctiveness of His Task."

"Not Ashamed—in His Continuing Preparations."

"Not Ashamed—in His Care of the Church."

"Not Ashamed—in His Spiritual Leadership of His People."

"Not Ashamed—in His Ministry of Healing."

"Not Ashamed—in His Relation to the World."

CHAPTER II

NOT ASHAMED—BECAUSE OF THE DISTINCTIVENESS OF HIS TASK

"...."I have appeared unto thee for this purpose, to make thee a minister ...."

Acts 26:16

What is a minister? A popular answer to this query speaks as follows:

Ministers come in assorted sizes and denominations. Some wear their collars frontward, others backward. Some wear vestments in the performance of their duties; some do not. But underneath these purely external manifestations there is a personality of deep understanding—a personality born, trained and educated to lead and enrich the lives of others.

Ministers are the spiritual leaders throughout life, from baptism to final rites. Joining man and woman together, ministers are master "knot tie-ers," liaisons of happiness!

Ministers are conservative in the way they live, yet spare nothing in the performance and devotion to their work. They are emblematic of that which cannot be seen, but only felt. They are mortals symbolic of an ideal, material leaders of the greatest of all intangibles.

At the very heart of such lines about the ministerial office is the truth of the spiritual distinctiveness of the task of the Christian minister. The Divine words spoken to Saul of Tarsus on that Damascus Road centuries ago have been repeated innumerable times since: "I have appeared unto thee for this purpose, to make thee a minister." (Acts 26:16.) There is something spiritually distinctive about the life and work of the minister.

The spiritual distinctiveness of the minister is seen, first of all, in the distinctiveness of his CALL to the ministry. It is true that the ways in which men are distinctively called to the ministry are as varied as their personalities are diverse. But in the case of every valid call to the Christian ministry, there is the personal consciousness on the part of the individual that he is being called distinctively, by a Higher Power, to do a distinctive work.

This realization of being called to the work of the ministry was ever-present in the spiritual consciousness of the Apostle Paul. He did not merely choose the ministry, nor did the circumstances of life summon him into it. Rather, he believed that God called him into it, that actually God put him into it. Hear him as he speaks of his Divine calling: "An apostle of Jesus Christ," (Titus 1:1); "called to be an apostle of Jesus Christ through the will of God," (I Corinthians 1:1); "called to be an apostle, separated unto the Gospel of God," (Romans 1:1); "an apostle of Jesus Christ by the will of God," (II Corinthians 1:1; Ephesians 1:1; Colossians 1:1; II Timothy 1:1); "an apostle of Jesus Christ by the commandment of God our Saviour," (I Timothy 1:1); "an apostle, (not of men, neither by man, but by Jesus Christ, and God the Father ...)" (Galatians 1:1); "... Christ Jesus our Lord, who hath ... counted me faithful, putting me into the ministry," (I Timothy 1:12); "whereunto I am ordained a preacher, and an apostle ...," (I Timothy 2:7); "I am appointed a preacher and an apostle and a teacher of the Gentiles," (II Timothy 1:11); "manifested His word through preaching, which is committed unto me according to the commandment of God our Saviour," (Titus 1:3).

In Colossians 1:25 Paul writes: "I am made a minister." He did not say that he made himself a minister nor did he mean that any human circumstances made him a minister. God made him a minister. Parents, a home, church, a college, a seminary, cannot make a minister. Even the church, considered in its most ideal concept, does not make a minister. Only Jesus Christ can make a minister. Ecclesiastical ordination only recognizes a minister already "made" by God. And so Paul reminds Timothy that the basis of their ministerial calling was not by virtue of "our works" but by virtue of God's purpose and grace. (II Timothy 1:9.)

This distinctiveness of the preacher's calling is summarized vividly in one of Paul's key phrases: "I, Paul, the prisoner of Jesus Christ", (Ephesians 3:1), and "I, therefore, the prisoner of the Lord," (Ephesians 4:1.) Even though these phrases refer actually to Paul's imprisonment in Rome, yet there is a deep spiritual meaning in them also. Paul was literally "a prisoner of Jesus Christ." Christ had captured him, all of him; and henceforth his entire life was lived in, for, with, and by the grace of Christ. Certainly, the spiritual application of this Pauline declaration suggests that the deepest, strongest, most sustaining motive in any man's calling to the ministry is a sense of being laid hold on, of being claimed by, of being made a captive, a prisoner of some Person beyond himself.

This personal consciousness of being distinctively

called to the work of the ministry has contemporary validations. A man in London who was giving his life to an unusually burdensome ministry was asked by a friend: "Why don't you run away from it all before you are broken by it?" The man immediately replied: "At times I would like to run away—I would like to run away from it all—but a strange Man on a Cross won't let me."

In speaking of his calling to the ministry, the Rev. William J. Hyde, of *Dig or Die, Brother Hyde* fame, declared in his own inimitable way:

> I knew that for me the ministry was the only profession to which I could give myself unreservedly. I thought about the folks in this town and their need for those things that only the Church can supply. The men engaged in growing wheat for the mills to turn into flour for bread—how much more they yearned for the Bread of Life. Engineers were talking about irrigation projects—how useless if the Water of Life did not flow freely, too. The merchants—how paltry their wares unless they realized they were secondary to the things of the Kingdom. People came to church because it had something unique to give them. I felt new joy at being one of the servants—even if the least—who served from this bountifully laden table. (p. 121)

I have a young friend who, during his senior year in an engineering course in a well-known university, experienced a call to the Christian ministry. Being the minister to his family at the time, I was hurriedly called into the confidence of the family when the first letter was received which told of the boy's new intentions for his life-work. So impressed was I by what he wrote his parents that I asked permission to copy some of the lines. I share them with you, and as you hear them, notice the constantly recurring note of the distinctiveness of being called to this particular work:

These last two weeks have been times of deep thought for me. When I came back to school after Christmas I was about half sure that I wanted to go into the ministry. Now I am almost positive.

I realize that you are not entirely "sold" on this idea, possibly for a number of reasons, which I will list below:

(1) Maybe I am making too hasty a decision, and would fit better in some other type of work.

(2) You may think the ministry is a field where people are under-paid and as such are pitied by their neighbors.

Those are the main things I can think of. Besides that, perhaps you think my $5,000 education (so far) has been, partially at least, wasted. Perhaps you are thinking of the continuing financial assistance I might need.

Assuming that the above might be some of your objections, let me explain what my answers would be.

The first, and most important thing, is whether I am making the right decision, and would fit into this work. It is the common conception of people, that if one is not "called" into the ministry, he will not be a success at the work. I am fairly sure that God wants me to do this type of thing, although I have heard no voices from heaven. I have told a few of my friends here about my ideas, and most of them think I am making a wise choice. After a church sermon about men going into the ministry, two of the boys here at the house asked me if I had thought about the ministry. These boys came up to me at different times, and neither knew that I had been thinking about doing the very thing they mentioned.

No other type of work appeals to me in the least any more. I feel that the main problems of the world are spiritual ones rather than material, and want to help improve the world by what little amount I can.

Now about the under-paid business. I don't measure my success in life with a material yardstick now. I believe in the Bible adage about building "treasures in heaven." Ministers, as a group, are the happiest people I know, and I believe this is because they are working for God and other people rather than for themselves. Aside from that, ministers are not the half-starved people they were fifty years ago. Most of them live comfortably.

Those are some of my ideas regarding the subject. Maybe you have noticed a change in tone even during this letter. At the start, I was "almost positive." Now that I have put my thoughts on paper, I am sure of my choice. In trying to sell you a bill of goods, I sold myself one. Please don't think that I, out of a clear blue sky, decided in this last one-half hour to become a minister. It's been on my mind since before Christmas vacation.

I hope you won't mind my making my choice without consulting you more about it than I did, but as I said when I was home, it was something I had to decide for myself.

How true it is—that in this matter of the Christian ministry those who are rightfully in it are personally conscious of having been distinctively called to this distinctive work. There is always present the inner personal conviction that God is speaking to me, that God wants me to do something specific for Him, that all my future "well-being," all of my sense of "wholeness" in the future, depend upon my obedience to this distinctive call. The "called" man understands the Apostle Paul when he writes: "For though I preach the Gospel, I have nothing to glory of: for necessity is laid upon me; yea, woe is unto me, if I preach not the Gospel!" (I Corinthians 9:16.)

The distinctiveness of the Christian ministry is seen, in the second place, in the distinctiveness of the PURPOSE to which a minister is called. On the Damascus Road Christ informed Saul of Tarsus: "I have appeared unto thee for this purpose." Did you ever stop and analyze the words which Christ spoke to Saul at this time, as they are recorded in the Apostle's own testimony before Agrippa? (Acts 26:13-18.)

At midday, O king, I saw in the way a light from heaven, above the brightness of the sun, shining round about me and them which journeyed with me.

And when we were all fallen to the earth, I heard a voice speaking unto me, and saying in the Hebrew tongue, Saul, Saul, why persecutest thou me? it is hard for thee to kick against the pricks.

And I said, Who art thou, Lord? And he said, I am Jesus whom thou persecutest.

But rise, and stand upon thy feet: for I have appeared unto thee for this purpose, to make thee a minister and a witness both of these things which thou hast seen, and of those things in the which I will appear unto thee;

Delivering thee from the people, and from the Gentiles unto whom now I send thee,

To open their eyes, and to turn them from darkness to light, and from the power of Satan unto God, that they may receive forgiveness of sins, and inheritance among them which are sanctified by faith that is in me."

Even a hurried analysis of these Pauline words will reveal a sixfold purpose to which a Christian minister is called. First, a Christian minister is called to be a CHRISTIAN MAN. The words "Rise, and stand upon thy feet," (Acts 26:16), suggest to me the picture of a real man. Paul's call to the ministry was, first of all, the call to the highest level of Christian manhood. Paul truly became "a man in Christ." For the minister to fail to be a Christian man, first of all, invalidates his call to the ministry. "Therefore if any man be in Christ, he is a new creature: old things are passed away; behold, all things are become new." (II

Corinthians 5:17.) Christ does not change a minister's personality when He calls him. But through an infusion of Divine Grace the natural endowments of mind and body and soul are purified and heightened. It is only in the "redeemed man" that the full development of the potential into the actual becomes a possibility.

Second, the Christian minister is called to be exactly what the name of his office implies—a MINISTER. "I have appeared unto thee for this purpose, to make thee a minister." (Acts 26:16.) A minister is a servant, a servant of people because he is, first of all, a servant of God. One is immediately reminded of Christ who "came not to be ministered unto, but to minister, and to give His life a ransom for many"; and of the Master's own words: "Ye know that they which are accounted to rule over the Gentiles exercise lordship over them; and their great ones exercise authority upon them. But so shall it not be among you: but whosoever will be great among you shall be your minister; and whosoever of you will be the chiefest, shall be servant of all." (Mark 10:42, 43.)

In the third place, the Christian minister is called to be a WITNESS. "I have appeared unto thee for this purpose, to make thee a witness." (Acts 26:16.) The function of witnessing is to relate what actually happens in personal experience. According to the Divine summons to Saul of Tarsus a Christian minister is a witness, both of the things which have already happened—"a witness both of those things which thou hast seen"—and of the things which continue to happen in spiritual experience to a minister—"and of those things in the which I will appear unto thee." Thus, in a very real way the vitality of a person's ministry is determined by his own spiritual experience; and the validity of past spiritual experiences is established by continuing experiences in which Christ Himself appears to the "called" man. We often remark facetiously about sermons that are dull and dry and somewhat ancient. If the Christian minister is truly a witness of what he has already experienced spiritually and of what he is continuing to experience in Divine revelation, then his ministry will be characterized continually by freshness, up-to-date-ness, radiance, life!

Fourth, the Christian minister is called to be a VICTOR—"delivering thee from the people, and from the Gentiles." (Acts 26:17.) The Christian minister is to experience a sense of triumph in his ministry. This triumph manifests itself at times in his being delivered from the fear of people—the fear of what people think and say, the fear of not being popular, the fear of being captive to others' attempted domination. Likewise, this triumph of the minister reveals itself in the personal consciousness that, in truth, "the wiles of the devil" and the evil schemes of wicked men cannot ultimately thwart the Divine purpose in one's ministry. Paul fought with beasts at Ephesus—but Paul's spiritual tombstone was not erected at Ephesus, for God's plan included Rome in the Pauline itinerary.

But being a Victor also means that the Christian minister is to share in a personal triumph of grace. "Now thanks be unto God, which always causeth us to triumph in Christ." (II Corinthians 2:14.) "Who shall separate us from the love of Christ? shall tribulation, or distress, or persecution, or famine, or nakedness, or peril, or sword? . . . Nay, in all these things we are more than conquerors through Him that loved us." (Romans 8:35, 37.) Such a continuing sense of spiritual triumph enabled Paul to declare confidently in his valedictory: "I have fought a good fight, I have finished my course, I have kept the faith: henceforth there is laid up for me a crown of righteousness." (II Timothy 4:7, 8.)

The Christian minister is, likewise, called as an APOSTLE—". . . the people, and the Gentiles, unto whom now I send thee." (Acts 26:17.) An apostle is one sent on a mission by one who has the authority to initiate such a mission. Jesus Christ sends ministers on the mission of redemption. And true ministers of Christ are more concerned about apostolic success than with apostolic succession in the fulfilment of such a mission.

The mission of the minister in the realm of redemption leads us to a consideration of the last aspect of the distinctiveness of the minister's calling. He is also called to be an EVANGELIST. "To open their eyes, and to turn them from darkness to light, and from the power of Satan unto God; that they may receive forgiveness of sins, and inheritance among them which are sanctified by faith that is in Me." (Acts 26:18) The Christian minister is the herald of the King, proclaiming the evangel of God's redeeming grace. Paul reminds Timothy that he will make full proof of his ministry only as he does the work of an evangelist. (II Timothy 4:5.) And the Apostle speaks of himself as an ambassador for Christ: "Now then we are ambassadors for Christ, as though God did beseech you by us: we pray in Christ's stead, be ye reconciled to God." (II Corinthians 5:20.)

And so we end our discussion of the distinctiveness of the minister's call to his work and of the purpose for which he is called. We move on to a third reason why the Christian minister is not ashamed because of the distinctiveness of his task, and we note the distinctive AUTHORITY of the minister.

The distinctive call of the minister, which we have already noted, is one aspect of the minister's distinctive authority. St. Paul rests the authority of his Divine call upon the appearance to him of the Risen Lord. Hear him as he tells the Corinthians: "And last of all He was seen of me also, as of one born out of due time. For I am the least of the apostles." (I Corinthians 15:8, 9.) Because ministers have this Divine call, there is the note of the spiritual authority behind them. In James Street's novel, *The Gauntlet*, his hero-preacher Wingo remarks, "And if she (his wife) dies, I'm through." Immediately his friend, the retired minister, the Rev. Mr. Honeycutt, replies, "No, no, Wingo, you are not through. You've touched the Cross and the sign is there. The imprint is on your hands and you can't wash it off. You are a preacher, and the people may revile you, but you belong to them because they belong to God."

The distinctive authority of the minister is also that of a continuing personal experience of Divine Grace. A study of the autobiographical sections in the prophecy of Jeremiah reveals that a vital factor in the spiritual authority of that prophet, and so of modern prophets, is the personal consciousness that what God has already done within one's own self He can do within and for others. But even more than this, there is the "prophet's" burning conviction that he must share with others, all through his life, this "good news" of God's grace, a spiritual reality which he continues to experience himself.

Perhaps there is a further aspect of distinctiveness in the authority of a minister, and that is to be found in what a person is willing to do and to endure in the fulfilment of his call to the ministry. The Apostle Paul testified that he bore in his body the marks of the Lord Jesus. (Galatians 6:17.) He also wrote to the Philippians reminding them that an essential requirement for knowing Jesus Christ is sharing in "the fellowship of His sufferings." (Philippians 3:10.)

When the Judaizers in the Church at Corinth disputed Paul's authority as a spiritual leader, one of the methods he used, in response, to establish his spiritual authority was to remind the people of all that he had suffered in his obedience to his Divine call. We recall his soul-stirring words:

Are they ministers of Christ? (I speak as a fool), I am more; in labors more abundant, in stripes above measure, in prisons more frequent, in deaths oft.

Of the Jews five times received I forty stripes save one.

Thrice was I beaten with rods, once was I stoned, thrice I suffered shipwreck, a night and a day I have been in the deep;

In journeyings often, in perils of water, in perils of robbers, in perils by mine own countrymen, in perils by the heathen, in perils in the city, in perils in the wilderness, in perils in the sea, in perils among false brethren;

In weariness and painfulness, in watchings often, in hunger and thirst, in fastings often, in cold and nakedness.

Besides those things that are without, that which cometh upon me daily, the care of all the churches. ((II Corinthians 11:23-28)

We must add a fourth reason for the distinctiveness of the Christian ministry—THE MINISTER OPERATES IN A DISTINCTIVELY SPIRITUAL REALM. Dr. J. B. Phillips, in his translation, puts these words into the mouth of Paul: "The truth is that, although of course we lead normal human lives, the battle we are fighting is on the spiritual level." (II Corinthians 10:3.) Paul tells the Ephesians that "we wrestle not against flesh and blood, but against principalities, against powers, the rulers of the darkness of this world, against spiritual wickedness in high places." (Ephesians 6:12.)

And because the minister operates in a distinctively spiritual realm he is given a distinctively spiritual power with which to do his work. The last words of our Saviour to His commissioned disciples were in relation to this Power which must possess them:

And, being assembled together with them, commanded them that they should not depart from Jerusalem, but wait for the promise of the Father, which, saith he, ye have heard of me.

For John truly baptized with water; but ye shall be baptized with the Holy Ghost not many days hence.

When they therefore were come together, they asked of him, saying, Lord, wilt thou at this time restore again the kingdom to Israel?

And he said unto them, It is not for you to know the times or the seasons, which the Father hath put in his own power.

But ye shall receive power, after that the Holy Ghost is come upon you: and ye shall be witnesses unto me both in Jerusalem, and in all Judea, and in Samaria, and unto the uttermost part of the earth. (Acts 1:4-8)

The Christian minister operates in a distinctively spiritual realm. He cannot live and work in this realm apart from being possessed by a unique spiritual power. That spiritual power, which is an absolute prerequisite, and without which the minister can only fail, is the Holy Spirit. Hence, every Christian minister is confronted today by the same question which Paul asked the elders of the church at Ephesus centuries ago: "Have ye received the Holy Spirit since you believed?" (Acts 19:2.)

The final aspect of the distinctiveness of the Christian ministry which we shall note is that of the distinctiveness of the minister's MESSAGE. At least three times in his epistles Paul speaks of the content of his preaching as "my Gospel." In the day when God shall judge the secrets of men by Jesus Christ according to my Gospel." (Romans 2:16.) "Now to Him that is of power to stablish you according to my Gospel." (Romans 16:25.) "Remember that Jesus Christ . . . was raised from the dead according to my Gospel." (II Timothy 2:8.)

It is evident that in his use of the term "my Gospel" Paul was not meaning to suggest any mere humanism, or naturalism, in the source of the Gospel. For in II Corinthians 2:12 he speaks of "Christ's Gospel;" and in Romans 15:16 he writes of the "Gospel of God;" and he tells the Thessalonians that the "Gospel came in the Holy Ghost." (I Thessalonians 1:5.) In fact, the

Apostle is dogmatic and vehement in his refutation of any kind of Gospel other than that whose source is Divine. (II Corinthians 11:4; Galatians 1:8, 11, 12.)

Rather must it be assumed that Paul was so utterly identified with and committed to the Gospel of God as it is in Jesus Christ that he thought of it in terms of "my" Gospel. Paul was what he was; Paul did what he was doing; Paul preached what he was preaching; Paul was willing to suffer what he was suffering; Paul hoped what he was hoping for—all because of the Gospel of Jesus Christ! For Paul to live was Christ— for the apostle Christ was life and life was Christ!

Isn't it wonderful that we, who follow in the spiritual tradition of the great apostle, can become so identified with the Gospel that we can speak of it as "my" Gospel? May I share with you, in very general terms, what is the content of "my" Gospel? As I share it, the distinctiveness of the Christian ministry becomes even more evident to me.

"My" Gospel is based on an historical fact—THE INCARNATION OF THE SON OF GOD. "The Word was made flesh, and dwelt among us, (and we beheld His glory, the glory as of the only-begotten of the Father) full of grace and truth." (John 1:14.) The Incarnation of Jesus Christ reaches its climax in His redemptive death upon the Cross for the sins of the world and His triumphant Resurrection from among the dead, and in His ascension into Heaven, where He now participates in an intercessory ministry for us before God.

"My" Gospel has an authentic textbook—THE

HOLY SCRIPTURES. "All Scripture is given by inspiration of God, and is profitable for doctrine, for reproof, for correction, for instruction in righteousness: that the man of God may be perfect, throughly furnished unto all good works." (II Timothy 3:16, 17.)

"My" Gospel is transmitted to men through a Divine Institution—THE CHRISTIAN CHURCH. "Upon this rock I will build My church: and the gates of hell shall not prevail against it." (Matthew 16:18.) " . . . Even as Christ also loved the church, and gave Himself for it: that He might sanctify and cleanse it with the washing of water by the word, that He might present it to Himself a glorious church, not having spot, or wrinkle, or any such thing; but that it should be holy and without blemish." (Ephesians 5:25-27.)

"My" Gospel is the only offer of ADEQUACY TO LIFE, which adequacy is realized in SPIRITUAL EXPERIENCE. "Therefore if any man be in Christ, he is a new creature: old things are passed away; behold, all things are become new." (II Corinthians 5:17). "I am come that they might have life, and that they might have it more abundantly." (John 10:10.) "Ye shall receive power, after that the Holy Ghost is come upon you." (Acts 1:8.) "My grace is sufficient for thee." (II Corinthians 12:9.)

"My" Gospel is committed to faithful men to proclaim—THE CHRISTIAN MINISTRY. We meet together under the influence of a deepening spiritual conviction—that the Christian ministry is a Divine vocation. Men are "separated unto the Gospel," (Romans 1:1), and are "put in trust with the Gospel."

(I Thessalonians 2:4.) J. B. Phillips expresses the sentiments of St. Paul in these words: "I myself have been made a minister of this same Gospel. For I am a minister of the Church by Divine commission, a commission granted to me for your benefit and for a special purpose: that I might fully declare God's Word." (Colossians 1:23, 25.)

Finally, "my" Gospel will have a GLORIOUS, ETERNAL CONSUMMATION. "And then shall appear the sign of the Son of man in heaven . . . and they shall see the Son of man coming in the clouds of heaven with power and great glory." (Matthew 24:30.) "And I saw a new heaven and a new earth." (Revelation 21:1.) "The kingdoms of this world are become the kingdoms of our Lord, and of His Christ; and He shall reign for ever and ever." (Revelation 11:15.)

And so we have hurriedly surveyed many of the aspects of the distinctiveness of the Christian ministry—the distinctiveness of the *Call* to the ministry, the distinctiveness of the *Purpose* to which a minister is called, the distinctiveness of the minister's *Authority*, the distinctiveness of the *Realm of Life* in which the minister operates, and the distinctiveness of the minister's *Message*.

In view of such a transcendent distinctiveness as that enjoyed by the Christian ministry, little wonder is it that spiritually-sensitive souls who have come under the influence of it have caught something of the distinctive glory of it all. Men of wisdom, in other callings, have understood and appreciated the uniqueness and relevance of the Christian ministry. Paul Elmer

More declared: "The priest is the only security we have against the complete invasion of a devastating materialism . . . . If I were young, I would preach." Lord Beaverbrook, one of the most influential men in Great Britain, once wrote:

> The evangelist is the man who has the greatest opportunity for doing good, and if I were in a position to influence the life of a sincere young man today, I would say to him, "Rather choose to be an evangelist than a Cabinet minister or a millionaire." When I was a young man I pitied my father for being a poor man and a humble preacher of the Word. Now that I am old I envy him, his life and career.

Some years ago when Dr. Samuel A. Eliot, son of President Charles W. Eliot, of Harvard College, was a young man, he was offered a position of large opportunity by the president of a great railway system. He refused the offer and entered the Christian ministry. Commenting on the decision, a friend of Harvard's noted president remarked, "I hear your son is entering the ministry. I had thought that he would go in for something real." Replied the distinguished Dr. Eliot, "He did go in for something real, the realest thing in the world, the chance to exercise influence upon the ruling sentiments of man."

Henry Morton Robinson, in his novel *The Cardinal* puts into the mouth of his hero, Stephen, words which to me are not only beautiful and moving but also a magnificent summary of the high calling of the minister:

> A priest is not a sociologist or politician or labor organizer. He is simply a mediator between God and man. (Of course, we Protestants accept only the definition of mediator in human terms.) He must keep his function pure, even though

the church is not indifferent to economic ills   Only poets can write poetry; only women can bear children. Only a priest can remind men that God forever was, is now, and— come hell, high water, or technology—always will be.

And just as truly those who have been influenced by the Christian ministry break forth into praiseful tributes of the spiritual distinctiveness of the ministry. Here are four illustrations, in poetic form, selected at random, which reveal this sense of appreciation and gratitude on the part of such folks:

THE PREACHER

He stands between the ever
And the now—
A slender, tender
Fragile coupling.

Through him pass the yearnings
Of the bruiséd and battered
Sons of earth—
The fervid hopes and prayers
Of cosmic neophytes
Perplexed and lost and lonely,
Clamoring for comfort
And hungering for courage
In communion with the soul of souls.

Through him comes, returning,
That strange mysterious flood
Of power—
The stream of hope and healing,
The word of everlasting wisdom,
The hand outreached . . . .

And there is none but Christ
With whom to share his anguish
As he finds himself
Too slender
Too tender
Too fragile.

—FRANKLIN D. ELMER, JR.

(Quoted in *The Christian Century*)

THE YOUNG PREACHER

He held the lamp of Truth that day
So low that none could miss the way;
And yet so high, to bring in sight
That picture fair—the world's great Light—
That gazing up, the lamp between,
The hand that held it scarce was seen.

He held the pitcher, stooping low
To lips of little ones below;
Then raised it to the weary saint,
And bade him drink, when sick and faint:
They drank—the pitcher thus between,
The hand that held it scarce was seen.

He blew the trumpet soft and clear,
That trembling sinners need not fear;
And then, with louder note and bold
To raze the walls of Satan's hold:
The trumpet coming thus between,
The hand that held it scarce was seen.

But when the Captain says, "Well done,
Thou good and faithful servant—come!
Lay down the pitcher and the lamp;
Lay down the trumpet—leave the camp:"
These weary hands will then be seen
Clasped in those pierced ones—naught between.

(*Written by a mother after her son's sermon
on the occasion of his ordination*)
(Quoted in *Now*)

IN DARKNESS

In darkness blacker than the darkest night,
I cried aloud to God for some small light
To see the Heavenly road
And rest my weary load.
He sent me you to set my steps aright.

Your kindness showed me that His spirit lives
In hearts of men, if we'll but see, and gives
The strength and power to win
O'er ignorance and sin.
He sent me you to show that He forgives.

You helped me up when grief caused me to fall
And shout to Heaven, "There is no God at all
To let such sorrow be."
His plan I could not see.
He sent me you to show Faith conquers all.

So now I must be witness unto Him
And teach my fellow-man whose faith is dim
The truths I've learned through you,
The Gospel old yet new.
He's sending me some other soul to win.

(*Written by one who had been greatly helped by
her minister*)

(*Quoted in "The Pastor's Journal"*)

LEGACY FROM A PASTOR

"No estate," the paper said,
"He had no cash or land."
But men shall treasure memories
Of how his healing hand
Had steadied them through darkened hours;
They think of how his prayer
Could set ajar the gates of Heaven;
They speak of how he'd share
His meager goods with all who came.
They see on paths he trod
Bright flowers of faith—this man so poor—
"So rich toward God!"

(*Leslie Savage Clark*)

(*Quoted in "The Christian Home"*)

And may I now speak personally? I shall forever remember the richness, the inspiration, of those moments, back in 1953, when I visited a devoted member of the Church, a beloved friend, who was almost dead from cancer. After I prayed for her she took my hand in her thin, disease-ravaged hands and prayed for me. She thanked God for my ministry and for what my ministry had meant to her personally. And then she prayed that God's richest blessing would ever be upon my future ministry, that others would be blessed as she had been. As I arose from my knees that afternoon, my very soul surged with emotion. I said to myself within the inner sanctuary of my heart: "What a high calling this is! There is none like it!"

Yes, men in the ministry feel the glory of it all! The Apostle Paul pictured himself as Christ's captive in God's triumphal march through the ages, and as Christ's captive he was selected to be an incense bearer in this Divine march of victory. (II Corinthians 2:24.)

A contemporary minister, who has chosen to remain anonymous, writes the following "glorious" words:

I am a preacher. I am one of the greatest line in the history of men. My fathers in God were Isaiah and Jeremiah, Peter and Paul, Luther and Walther. My line reaches back beyond the Cross to the days before the flood came over the earth. Only because of the church I serve and the Word I preach does God permit the world to roll on its way. I have watched men step quietly through the last gate because I had been permitted to show them the way. There are men and women, and children, too, before the throne of Heaven today who are my children. They are there because God let me bring them there. The saints of the church are my joy and the sinners are my burden. I am an ambassador of the King of kings. My lips are among the few left in the world that speak truth. I, almost alone among men, deal day after day with eternal things. I am the last echo of a far voice that forever calls men Home. I am the hand of the Bridegroom, the shadow of the Cross, the trumpet of the King. Neither obscurity nor unpopularity can rob me of my glory. It is not my own, but the reflected glory of Him whose free and happy slave I am. (Quoted in **The American Lutheran**)

Hugh Price Hughes, eminent British clergyman and Methodist leader of a past generation, whose brilliant natural endowments would have been an ornament in any profession, never regretted his "high calling" to the work of the Christian ministry. A little over forty years after his entering the ministry, as he was riding on the top of an omnibus with a relative past Westminster and the Houses of Parliament, the thoughts of the two gravitated by common consent to the scene that they knew was being enacted within the lighted House.

"You should have been there," said the relative. "What, what, dear? Where should I be?" "In Parliament." "Ah, Parliament, why?" "Well, because you would have been a leader there." Then, after a few moments, Hugh Price Hughes commented, "There is nothing that I would rather be than a minister of the Gospel of Jesus Christ."

Dr. F. E. Davison, for more than forty years a Christian minister, and who was elected to the presidency of the International Convention of Disciples of Christ, has recently published a book entitled *I Would Do It Again.* So convincing is the volume that one of its reviewers wrote: "It gave me the uneasy feeling that perhaps I have been wasting my time all these years by being a university professor and an editor.

Maybe I had better start over and be the pastor of a church."

"Dig or Die Brother" Hyde, a pioneer Methodist preacher in the Dakota Territory, shares with us in these moving lines from his autobiography the sense of glory which was his as a Christian minister:

And so I finished out the first week in Dakota Territory and Sunday arrived. As I climbed on to Queen's back and put my Bible and sermon notes in a small saddle bag I experienced a great thrill—I had joined the long procession of circuit riders who from the days of Asbury, through Shadford, Peter Cartwright, Eggleston and others, had carried the Message out beyond the confines of established churches. It didn't make any difference if I was the last and the least of them all. I had a tremendous sense of "belonging" and that adds immeasurably to a man's own slender resources. (p. 59)

But "called" men, in the midst of the "glory" of the Christian ministry, realizing the sobering responsibility of such a call from God, to such a distinctive task, have "shuddered reverently" and have "thrown their whole weight" upon God for strength and guidance. A young friend of mine, in a letter, revealed the inner thoughts of his mind and heart as he approached the holy moment of ordination:

But when it came (the decision to ordain him a deacon in Protestant Episcopal Church- .   I was not prepared spiritually   I stayed up most of the night   trying to prepare for the service. . . .

Throughout the service I felt terrifically impressed and depressed. I saw clearly what God demands, and I knew how pathetically short I fell. I was especially convicted of pride and lack of love. I saw how this affected all my relationships in this community. I understood something of how God deals with these things, and I knew clearly that to be a minister in the church is to be a humble channel for God's love, and I was everything and anything but this. I felt though it were only cowardice that kept me from running away when they asked in the service if any one knew good reason why I should not be ordained. I thought even the stones must shout out the reasons that I so clearly understood in my heart.

The holy awe of the Christian minister in the presence of God and of the Divine call which is his, is most eloquently revealed in Martin Luther's famed sacristy prayer:

O Lord God, dear Father in heaven, I am, indeed, unworthy of the office and ministry in which I am to make known Thy glory and to nurture and to serve this congregation.

But since Thou hast appointed me to be a pastor and teacher, and the people are in need of the teachings and the instructions, O be Thou my helper and let Thy holy angels attend me.

Then if Thou art pleased to accomplish anything through me to Thy glory and not to mine or to the praise of men, grant me, out of Thy pure grace and mercy, a right understanding of Thy Word and that I may, also, diligently perform it.

O Lord Jesus Christ, Son of the living God, Thou Shepherd and Bishop of our souls, send Thy Holy Spirit that He may work with me, yea, that He may work in me to will and to do through Thy divine strength according to Thy good pleasure. Amen.

Truly, because of the distinctiveness of his task, the Christian minister is "a workman that needeth not to be ashamed."

CHAPTER III

NOT ASHAMED—IN HIS CONTINUING PREPARATIONS

" . . . give attendance to reading . . ." (I Timothy 4:13.)
"Neglect not the gift that is in thee . . . Meditate upon these things; give thyself wholly to them; that thy profiting may appear to all." (I Timothy 4:14, 15) *"Redeeming the time . . ."* (Ephesians 5:16) *". . . be instant in season, out of season . . "* (II Timothy 4:2)

When an individual enters upon the work of the Christian ministry, in a very real sense he is already a prepared man. To begin with, the Divine factor always enters into the preparation of a true minister. God reminded young Jeremiah: "Before I formed thee in the belly I knew thee; and before thou camest forth out of the womb I sanctified thee, and I ordained thee a prophet unto the nations." (Jeremiah 1:5.)

And how varied and extensive are the human elements involved in the making of ministers. One of the schools that prepares ministers is the home. Usually in the making of a priestly Samuel there is a Hannah; Elkanah being often a modest partner. And who will ever fully understand the evangelical leadership of John Wesley apart from his mother, Susannah, and his father, Samuel?

The local church is also a school in the making of ministers. Often the pastor is the principal teacher, and participation in youth work has afforded many valuable lessons. Then comes the undergraduate college. Originally many of our great colleges and universities not only had ministerial beginnings but ministerial purposes. And what would a minister's life and activity be like apart from the training of the theological seminary? Contemporary ministers must have their School of the Prophets.

But admitting the fact that when a Christian minister begins his work he is definitely a prepared man, it is just as true to declare that the preparation of a minister is never completed. It is a continuing preparation. If at any precise period of time the minister would presume to affirm, or even to believe, that at long last "my preparation for the ministry is completed," at that very instant there could be heard the sound of the "death rattle" in relation to the effectiveness of such a ministry. And, so, the true preparation of a minister is made possible when the minister realizes that in a very real sense his preparation will never be completed but at the same time he "presses on" to make his preparation as complete as humanly possible.

I believe that the continuing preparation of a minister is to be realized in The Disciplined Life. Someone has suggested that Jesus' ·parable of the Wise Virgins (Matthew 25) has this meaning for preachers: the "vessels" represent a minister's life; the "lamp" his actual ministry; and the "oil" signifies a minister's discipline. In our thinking together I propose to speak of the continuing preparation of the Christian minister under these three headings: (1) the Discipline of the Self; (2) the Discipline of the Mind; (3) the Discipline of the Spirit.

THE DISCIPLINE OF THE SELF

St. Paul reminded young Timothy that he must always take heed unto himself (I Timothy 4:16). In the last analysis, the authority of a man's ministry is no greater than the authority of the self, of the life, behind the ministry. The minister's life is always the greatest sermon he ever preaches. The words of St. Francis of Assisi to his friend who traveled with him on a silent "preaching mission" through the little Italian town are almost immortal: "Brother, we preached as we walked." A ministry of growing power must be one of enlarging life, of expanding experience.

The minister himself, the minister's self, is of basic importance to one's ministry. In his book, *Growing Spiritually*, E. Stanley Jones points out that there are twenty-eight things spoken of in II Corinthians 6:4-10 proving Paul was a "true minister of God." And every single one is a moral and spiritual quality of his life and action; there is not one mention of his performing any miracle. (p. 120)

In a moving sermon St. Chrysostom reminds his readers that "none can injure one who does not injure himself." Think of what this means to a Christian minister. None can injure a minister's ideal of the ministry unless he lowers it himself. None can injure a minister's spirit in the ministry unless he corrupts it himself. None can injure the influence of a minister's activities unless he limits it himself. None can injure a minister's glory of being in the ministry unless he is unresponsive himself.

A contemporary writer, John Stevenson, declared recently:

"Many people have the ambition to succeed; they may even have special aptitude for their job. And yet they do not move ahead. Why? Perhaps they think that since they can master the job, there is no need to master themselves."

The continuing preparation of the minister truly demands the Discipline of the Self. But this is not accomplished as easily as it is declared, for there are many things involved in a minister's Discipline of the Self.

Basically, the Discipline of the Self demands a spiritual experience. This is what the Apostle Paul is talking about when he declares: "I am crucified with Christ: nevertheless I live; yet not I, but Christ liveth in me: and the life which I now live in the flesh I live by the faith of the Son of God, who loved me, and gave Himself for me." (Galatians 2:20.) Unless the carnal self be dead, Christ cannot reign. Robert Barclay, one of the early Quaker theologians, expresses a timeless spiritual truth in these words:

"For he (the devil) well knoweth that so long as SELF bears rule, and the Spirit of God is not the principal and chief actor, man is not put out of his reach; so therefore he can accompany the priest to the altar, the preacher to the pulpit, the zealot to his prayers, yea, the doctor and professor of divinity to his study, and there he can cheerfully suffer him to labor and work among his books, yea, and help him to find out and invent subtile distinctions and quiddities by which both his mind and others through him may be kept from heeding God's Light in the conscience and waiting upon Him. (**An Apology for the True Divinity** pp. 352-353)

In Henry M. Robinson's novel *The Cardinal* we find Deegan, the building contractor, speaking to Stephen, the hero, in language like this:

Once, I thought you were ambitious, Stephen. I see now that the fire of the Holy Ghost has burned that ambition right down to cinders. But did you know that cinder blocks make the best building material? Stuff that's passed through fire to ash can't be burned by anything else. Master contractors know that.

Truly we Wesleyans understand, in an intimate way, all this insistence upon a spiritual experience in which the carnal self is crucified and the total self is cleansed and filled by the Spirit of God, for we are the inheritors of John Wesley's cherished doctrine of Christian Perfection. When we are most loyal to our spiritual heritage we are most faithful in our advocacy of the great Scripture doctrine of Sanctification, a spiritual experience realizable in this life. And we believe in the Deeper Life for individuals because they are Christians, not primarily because they are ministers. What a shame, to use the words of W. E. Sangster, that we Methodists have permitted ourselves to be robbed of this "spiritual treasure" by others who have often made a caricature out of it.

The Discipline of the Self demands a continuing wholehearted dedication to the work of the Christian ministry. This wholehearted devotion to one's task will be evident, even if one is tempted at times "to feel robbed" because he finds himself in the ministry. I once heard a minister give a very unusual interpretation of the Parable of the Good Samaritan. Among other things he said, "Suppose the minister should think of himself as the victim in the parable." He then proceeded to speak of five ways in which a minister may be tempted to feel robbed: (1) no time for himself; (2) little time for his family; (3) his reputation is constantly at the "whimsical mercy" of the public; (4) his often inadequate material resources; (5) he is often "passed by" in the thinking of others just because he is a minister. But the minister learns to discipline himself in the direction of knowing that no true servant of God is ever really "robbed." In addition to all the marvelous satisfactions of a minister's earthly life there are tremendous "treasures in heaven" being laid up.

This wholehearted dedication to the work of the Christian ministry, likewise, includes the devotion of all one's time to the work. Every minister entering a Methodist Annual Conference is asked, among other things, this question: "Are you determined to employ all your time in the work of God?" A preacher in the western country applied to General Jackson for an office of some character. At the time he applied, the general did not know the applicant was a preacher, and he very politely promised that he would think of his claims, and weigh them. The preacher saw the general a few days after, and renewed his application. The general in the meantime had gotten information that the applicant was a preacher of the Gospel. The general asked him if he was a preacher of the Gospel; he answered he was. "Well," said the general, "if you discharge the duties of that office, which is better than any I can confer, you will have no time to discharge the duties of any that I can give; you will, therefore, excuse me for advising you to return home, and attend to that, without being burdened with any other, that you may be enabled to account hereafter for your stewardship in this world."

For the minister the Discipline of the Self must always be in the direction of Christ-likeness. It means a life that is "growing in grace and in the knowledge of Jesus Christ." It manifests itself in an exemplary pattern of Christian living. A Christ-like ministry demands, first of all, Christ-likeness of soul and character within the person who would exercise that quality of ministry.

Lin Yutang reminds us of life's inevitable demand for spiritual self-discipline when he writes these words about Chinese artists:

Calm and harmony distinguish Chinese art, and calm and harmony come from the soul of the Chinese artist. The Chinese artist is a man who is at peace with nature, who is free from the shackles of society and from the temptations of gold, and whose spirit is deeply immersed in mountains and rivers and other manifestations of nature. Above all, his breast must brood no ill passions, for a good artist, we strongly believe, must be a good man. He must first of all "chasten his heart" or "broaden his spirit," chiefly by travel and by contemplation. This is the severe training we impose on the Chinese painter. **(My Country and My People)**

Spiritual self-discipline for the minister makes possible the continuing operation of the Grace of God upon the life of the minister. The minister, like the people he exhorts, must grow in grace. The Grace of God in the minister's heart and life is more than an initial act; it is a life, a developing life, a maturing experience. Such growing spiritual life means the deepening of faith, the enlarging of love, the intensifying of hope.

How may a minister help himself become disciplined in the direction of increasing Christ-likeness? (I speak now not from the standpoint of spiritual devotional aids, which will be mentioned later, but in reference to personal spiritual discipline.) I would like to suggest that the minister keep a disciplined "check" on himself by judging himself regularly in reference to two great Scripture declarations of the Apostle Paul—his discussion of "The Fruit of the Spirit", (Galatians 5:22, 23) and his "Hymn of Love," (I Corinthians 13).

Let the minister confront his soul regularly with his responsibility for manifesting "the Fruit of the Spirit."

"The fruit of the Spirit is LOVE"

Am I becoming more loving every day?

"The fruit of the Spirit is JOY"

Is my life characterized by an increasing and contagious radiance?

"The fruit of the Spirit is PEACE"

Am I maturing in my possession and manifestation of spiritual serenity and personal poise?

"The fruit of the Spirit is LONGSUFFERING"

Am I finding it easier to manifest patience?

"The fruit of the Spirit is GENTLENESS"

Does my ministry abound in kindliness because my heart is kind?

"The fruit of the Spirit is GOODNESS"

Do I know myself basically to be a good person intent upon becoming a better person?

"The fruit of the Spirit is FAITH"

Do I understand what Job meant when he said, "Though He slay me, yet will I trust Him"?

"The fruit of the Spirit is MEEKNESS"

Am I humble, in the New Testament sense of the word?

How the minister must beware of pride. It has been called "the first sin, the greatest of temptations to a minister's intellect." The minister's stature must be made small before men that it may be great in the eyes of God. So important is humility to the work of a minister that St. Francis wrote:

"It were well if we could find some great and heavy weight that we might ever hang about our necks, in order that it might ever bear us down, to wit, that it might ever make us humble ourselves."

What tragic words are these uttered by a wise minister about his talented but proud colleague: "It seemed to me he could become a great man if he could be persuaded he was not God's greatest gift to The Methodist Church."

"The fruit of the Spirit is TEMPERANCE"

Do I possess a self-control which is Christ-like? Would it be said of me, as Willa Cather said of a friend, "He had beautiful manners with himself even when he was alone?"

Or let the minister be guided by Paul's Hymn of Love, as a life-discipline.

"Love suffereth long, and is kind; love envieth

not; love vaunteth not itself, is not puffed up.

"Doth not behave itself unseemly, seeketh not her own, is not easily provoked, thinketh no evil;

"Rejoiceth not in iniquity, but rejoiceth in the truth;

"Beareth all things, believeth all things, hopeth all things, endureth all things.

"Love never faileth."

Now re-read Paul's words, substituting your own name for the word "love." ——————————— suffers long? ——————————— is kind?? ———————————— envies not???

The Discipline of the Self, likewise, means a personality so disciplined in its responses to life that those responses will be distinctly Christian. In the hour of *temptation* the minister must respond as a Christian man. And, don't forget it, the minister is a severely-tempted man. Not only is he subject to the ordinary temptations of manhood, but he is also confronted by the hazardous temptations that are peculiar to his calling. In the hour of temptation he must not fall. He must discipline himself, by God's grace, to permit God's grace always to triumph in the time of temptation. "How can I do this great wickedness and sin against God?" was Joseph's watchword. And Daniel purposed in his heart that he would not defile himself with "the king's meat." I have thought often that there are a great many areas in a preacher's experience where he has to erect and strictly observe "No Trespassing" signs.

Every minister realizes the need of heeding these words of Paul:

"Athletes will take tremendous pains—for a fading crown of leaves. But our contest is for an eternal crown that will never fade. I run the race then with determination. I am no shadow-boxer, I really fight! I am my body's sternest master, for fear that when I have preached to others I should myself be disqualified." (I Corinthians 9:24 ff, Phillips.)

In the time of *difficulties* the minister must reveal himself to be a true follower of the Son of God. All kinds of difficulties cross the path of ministers. Sometimes difficulty comes under the guise of the demand for a minister to spend most of his time doing the things he considers the least important and most irksome. A recent survey finds ministers complaining of being compelled to do such things as "paper work," "running the mimeograph," "attending too many purposeless meetings," and "dealing with demanding people."

At other times difficulty manifests itself in ridicule and opposition from the outside world. Read what Paul said about his being confronted by such difficulties as a minister. In the words of J. B. Phillips, Paul said that he was "last in the procession of mankind," "a public spectacle," considered a "fool," "weak," an object of "contempt;" he was "knocked about," "cursed by men" who made his life miserable;" considered as the "world's rubbish," "the scum of the earth." (I Corinthians 4:8 ff.)

On still other occasions difficulty manifests itself

in ugly problems that defy immediate solution, and in burdensome perplexities which harass and threaten to overwhelm a minister. But in the midst of it all the minister will learn to triumph through the inexhaustible resources of Divine Grace. I well remember one such occasion among others in my own ministry. One problem in particular was plaguing me in my administration of the church. I became exhausted and disheartened and found myself almost at "the end of my rope," so to speak. Then I attended a church service in which the beautiful hymn "My Faith Looks Up to Thee" was sung. During the singing of the hymn certain words leaped at me with new meaning and such spiritual forcefulness that I was lifted to new heights of spiritual victory. Let me share with you the transforming impact of that spiritual hymn upon me as a minister that night:

> "My faith LOOKS UP to Thee
> Thou Lamb of Calvary,
> Saviour Divine;
> Now HEAR ME while I pray,
> Take all my guilt away,
> O let me from this day
> Be WHOLLY THINE.
>
> "May THY RICH GRACE impart
> STRENGTH to my FAINTING HEART
> MY ZEAL INSPIRE:
> As Thou hast died for me

O may MY LOVE to Thee
Pure, warm and changeless be,
A LIVING FIRE.

The minister's disciplined responses to life, also, include the mastery of his moods. Any person whose work binds him inextricably with the lives of countless others is subject to drastic moods, particularly the mood of discouragement which manifests itself especially when things are not working out the way he knows that they should. I think of the great leader Moses. At one time he would express his willingness to die for his people. (Exodus 32:31, 32.) At another time he wanted to die to get away from the people. (Numbers 11:11-15.)

How true it is that the minister whose ministry helps people get the best of moods has his turn at trying to conquer them. Do you remember Moffatt's translation of Job 4:3-5: "You have yourself set many right, and put strength into feeble souls; your words have kept men on their feet, the weak-kneed you have nerved. But now that your own turn has come, you droop; it touches you close, and you collapse."

Sometimes the minister's mood of discouragement almost reaches the place of the temptation to regret that he ever entered the ministry. Albert Schweitzer was once tempted to regret his life decision for Christian service. But he triumphed as "seeing Him who is invisible." My mind returns again and again to the scene in *The Cardinal* when the young priest falls victim to the mood of discouragement and walks up-and-down the edge of the New England ice pond, overgrown with weeds and rushes, pensively seeking some solution to his dilemma. And each time that he is alone he hears again the wise words of his trusted friend:

> You will all be assailed . by the very real temptation to believe that you have been forsaken by God—that your priesthood is in vain, and that the weight of mortal grief and sin is more than you can bear. In the midst of your anguish you will ask of Him a sign, some visible ray of His unchanging light in a world of hideous darkness. I am sorry to say that this visible sign will rarely be given. The burning bush of Moses, the jewel-encrusted dove of Theresa, the Tolle lege of Augustine—these are no longer the style, as in the simpler days of saint and prophet. The light will be interior; you must look for it within.

Perhaps several hurried suggestions will help a minister triumph over the deadly mood of discouragement. First, the mood of discouragement often is the psychological reaction to extreme mental and physical fatigue. Let the minister be sure that in such an hour he is adequately rested. Second, discouragement often results from an impractical idealism and an illogical attempt at perfectionist activity. I have often been tempted to cry out: "O hopeless idealist that I am: who shall deliver me from the bondage of believing that in this life all ideals can become realities!" Ministers need to make a valid distinction between philosophical idealism and moral responsibility. Just because a minister knows all that can be done, and wants to do it, it does not necessarily imply *oughtness* in the doing of it all, for the doing of it all may transcend the bounds of human capacity and of possibility, particularly where other volitions are involved.

Often the Divine Voice has to speak in some personal way to lift a minister out of discouragement. At one point in the ministry of the Rev. Stephen Olin, one of the shining lights of New England Methodism, he became greatly discouraged, and attempted to leave his work.

A significant dream relieved him. He thought he was working with a pickaxe on the top of a basaltic rock. His muscular arm brought down stroke after stroke for hours; but the rock was hardly indented. He said to himself, "It is useless; I will pick no more." Suddenly, a stranger of dignified mien stood by his side, and thus spoke to him: "You will pick no more?" "No." "Were you not set to this task?" "Yes." "And why abandon it?" "My work is in vain; I make no impression on the rock." Solemnly the stranger replied: "What is that to you? Your duty is to pick, whether the rock yields or not. Your work is in your own hands: the result is not. Work on!" He resumed his task. The first blow was given with almost superhuman force, and the rock flew into a thousand pieces. He awoke, returned to his work, and a great revival followed. From that day, he never had a temptation to give up his commission.

In the midst of all his moods, be they constructive or negative, let the true minister remind himself that his is a life-calling. At a reception given me in one of my churches, upon my return from Annual Conference, one of the officials arose and said: "If I could have my way I would have my minister 'sentenced for life' to this church." "Sentenced for life"—take it in its highest spiritual connotation—the minister is "sentenced for life" in this high calling. Moods come and go—the sense of the high calling must never grow dim.

May I hurriedly mention another thing which I believe to be involved in the Discipline of the Self? It is the discipline of being one's self. Ministers, like true artists, should not copy others. There devolves upon the minister the discipline of being utterly natural, provided that naturalness means being one's best self. The temptation to try to be other than one's own self must always be resisted. And let the minister beware of succumbing to the temptation to disparage one's self because of a sense of inferiority in the presence of another who is judged to be, and perhaps rightly so, far better and more gifted than he knows himself to be.

All of this discussion about the Discipline of the Self reaches a logical climax in declaring that the minister's life and ministry must give evidence of that quality of spiritual life made possible only through the disciplined employment of devotional habits. I think immediately of such "holy habits" of the Christian life as Bible-reading, meditation, prayer. When all is said and done a minister's spiritual life is no stronger than the weakest link in his devotional life.

And how utterly imperative it is for the minister to be continually in the best state of spiritual health. In the little community in Scotland where Thomas Carlyle lived, the people were seeking a new minister. When his advice about a new minister was asked, Carlyle said: "What this parish needs before everything else is a preacher who knows God other than by hearsay."

The only way to kill a minister is to kill his experience of God. When a preacher listens to God, then people will listen to him. If a minister doesn't take time to listen to God, people will not take time to listen to him. People always go to a fire, and if one gets started in the minister's soul, they will flock to see the great sight.

I regret that I do not have time to discuss in detail the devotional habits of the minister. May I suggest that every young minister read what Dr. Albert E. Day has to say about the spiritual art of meditation in his volume entitled, *An Autobiography of Prayer?*

No "holy habit" is more important for the minister than that of prayer. Let these words from Andrew Murray make an indelible spiritual imprint upon the minister's mind and heart:

What is the reason many thousands of Christian workers in the world have not greater influence? Nothing save this— the prayerlessness of their service. In the midst of all their zeal in the study and in the work of the Church, of all their faithfulness in preaching and conversation with the people, they lack that ceaseless prayer which has attached to it the sure promise of the Spirit, and the power from on high. It is nothing but the sin of prayerlessness which is the cause of the lack of a powerful spiritual life. . The indispensable thing is not preaching, not pastoral visitation, not church work, but fellowship with God in prayer until we are clothed with power from on high!

A western rancher had asked the district superintendent that a pastor be assigned to his community. "How big a man do you want?" the district superintendent asked. "Well, Elder," the wiry man of tan replied, "we're not overly particular, but when he's on his knees we'd like to have him reach heaven." John Wesley said to his preachers: "Study yourself to death; then pray yourself alive again."

May I strongly urge that every minister read and re-read and thoroughly digest the rich spiritual contents of E. M. Bounds' little volume *Power Through Prayer*. It is truly a spiritual gold mine!

Permit me to make just one suggestion about the minister's personal Bible study. Occasionally it might be profitable to read devotionally a Book in the Bible primarily from the viewpoint of what it reveals about the ministry. In my devotional study of the Bible I have followed this method twice—in my study of the Prophecy of Jeremiah and of Paul's Letters to the Corinthians.

Take a look at what I discovered about the Christian ministry in my devotional study of First and Second Corinthians. Each chapter in those two Pauline Epistles revealed to me an aspect of the minister's life and work:

I Corinthians
1 The Minister and Jesus Christ
2 The Minister and the Holy Spirit
3 The Minister and other ministers
4 The Minister and himself
5 The Minister and church administration
6 The Minister and his example
7 The Minister and his personal relationships
8 The Minister and his privileges
9 The Minister and his reward

10 The Minister and the lessons of history
11 The Minister and the Sacraments
12 The Minister and spiritual gifts
13 The Minister and love
14 The Minister and his effectiveness
15 The Minister and the resurrection
16 The Minister and his co-laborers

II Corinthians 1 The Minister and his trustworthiness
2 The Minister and discipline
3 The Minister and the new dispensation
4 The Minister and his methods
5 The Minister and his personal consciousness of immortality
6 The Minister and the blamelessness of his ministry
7 The Minister and his comfort
8 The Minister and stewardship
9 The Minister and church finances
10 The Minister and self-judgment
11 The Minister and his rightful dignity
12 The Minister and his weaknesses
13 The Minister and his fondest hopes for his people

THE DISCIPLINE OF THE MIND

And so we must close our discussion on the Discipline of the Self, which is an integral part of The Disciplined Life. But we proceed to emphasize the further truth that there must also be the Discipline of the Mind in the continuing preparations of the minister. It is only as the minister disciplines his mind along the paths of alertness, receptivity, orderliness and spiritual creativity that he will rise above that all-too-general tendency for a minister to be dull and colorless and oftentimes tragically ineffective.

I heard of a preacher whose congregation flinches against his time-worn theme: the sin of staying away from church on Sunday. One Monday not long ago this preacher buttonholed one of his young parishioners with the greeting that he had missed him in church the preceding day. He then launched into the subject of Sunday's sermon: "Son, you don't stay away from the movies because it's too much trouble to get dressed, or you were out late the night before. Now, that's true, isn't it?" "Yes, preacher, it is," agreed the unabashed young man. "And it is also true you don't go if you've already seen the picture."

W. E. Gladstone's rule for his mind is a worthy ideal for all ministers: he never allowed his exports to exceed his imports. Asked the secret of his power as a preacher, a Negro minister declared, "It's simple. I reads myself full, I thinks myself clear, I prays myself hot, and then I lets myself go."

To discipline the mind effectively requires both an understanding of and a conformity to the laws of the mind. May I state very simply the basic laws which govern the operation of the mind. There are at least four such fundamental laws: (1) Food—the mind must be fed with truth; (2) Exercise—the mind must exercise itself in the use of the truth it already possesses and in the quest for new truth. I think often of my minister-friend who in offering to give me one of Reinhold Niebuhr's books remarked: "I couldn't get beyond the first paragraph." But the mind when it truly exercises itself will get beyond the first paragraph, even if it takes a long time to do it.

(3) Concentration—the mind cannot function efficiently apart from the discipline of periods of concentration. Too many ministers, to use the words of Simeon Stylites, could qualify for the Order of Holy Grasshoppers. They have little time for hoping in the Lord—they are so busy "hopping in the Lord." A minister's daughter once asked what it meant for bishops to be "concentrated." Maybe she had something there. Certainly there are times when concentration is consecration. (4) Relaxation—just as the mind must have periods of concentration, so it must have alternate periods of relaxation. And, of course, the best relaxation is never to be found in a cessation from activity but in a change of activity. An active mind will ever be active, but we must discipline it to be active in different directions, so that the result will be a mind that knows how to renew itself and refresh itself and remain creative and fertile.

I would like to discuss this significant area of the Discipline of the Mind in the minister's continuing preparations under three main headings: (1) The minister and planning; (2) the minister and his study tools; and (3) the minister and preparing to preach.

The Minister and Planning

My formula is stated as simply as this: I plan my

year. I plan my week. I plan my day. I use summer opportunities to assist me in my planning.

I PLAN MY YEAR. Before the beginning of each church year a minister should have a general master plan for the church and his ministry for that year. Knowing the emphases to be observed in the church for the new year, some of these emphases traditional to the general church year and others to the particular local chruch, and some of them selected as the result of a church Planning Conference or of his own independent decision, he should plan his ministerial activities and his preaching accordingly. Just one illustration must suffice: how much more effective it is for a minister to be preaching on Christian Stewardship just before the Every Member Canvass than two weeks after it is completed.

I PLAN MY WEEK. When a minister plans his week he must build the plan around the scheduled events of the week. There are regularly-scheduled events in the family life, in the pastor's life, in the church life, and in the community life. Then each week has its own specially-scheduled events. There are special committee meetings, special counseling conferences, special pastoral visits, funerals, weddings, baptisms, and the like. It is well for a minister, as much as it is humanly possible, to see the week in its entirety as he begins its activity. Such a plan may help the minister to refuse to engage in more activities than one week permits.

I PLAN MY DAY. I get a better start each morning when I have somewhat of a plan for the entire day.

When I was a young preacher in much smaller churches I attempted to follow some of the daily schedules
prescribed for preachers as suggested in theological
seminary. Such a plan is worked out on practically an
hourly basis: an hour for Bible study, an hour for
theology, an hour for philosophy, an hour for corre-
spondence, etc., etc. The day has long passed since such
a detailed daily schedule has proved practical to me.
All other things being equal, I will now settle for the
following daily schedule: in the study in the morning;
early afternoon in the church office; the rest of the
afternoon in pastoral visitations; and the evening re-
served for administrative and social activities. What
about my family? Oh, well, they seem to love me any-
way! (I should add that I do not believe in a seven-day
workweek for the minister. "Six days shalt thou labor
and do all thy work." Saturday is the day I try to keep
for myself and for the family.)

I USE SUMMER OPPORTUNITIES FOR PLAN-
NING. The summer season, when church work is
usually lighter in many areas, is a wonderful occasion
for the minister to plan for his church activities and
for his preaching during a new year. It is also a splendid opportunity for the minister to give some extra
time and attention to his "workshop." Files can be
brought up-to-date, books can be perused a little more
carefully, and a host of other study interests can be
catered to more adequately.

The Minister and His Study Tools

Every artist and every artisan has his own cherished tools. Just so, the minister has his "tools" which

must be collected, organized, made accessible, and kept up-to-date. As the slogan goes, "You can't do today's job with yesterday's tools and be in business tomorrow."

Even though ideas and all those things which stimulate ideas must be reckoned as "study tools" for a minister, I want to limit this discussion to those rather external mechanical things which are found in a minister's study. I am thinking of such objects as books and bookshelves, magazines and magazine tables, files and filing cabinets.

I love books and as a result I have accumulated many of them. Therefore my responsibility is to know at any time just where to find a particular book when needed. I have decided that the best method to have every volume handy at all times is to arrange one's library topically. All books on Theology should be in one section; all books in the field of Church History should be in another section; all books on the Life and Teachings of Jesus Christ in another section; all books of Sermons in still another section, and so forth.

I use the following subjects for the arrangement of books in my library: General Church History, Methodism, Missions, Theology, Ecumenical Church, Philosophy, Psychology, Healing, Comparative Religions, Sermons, The Minister and Ministerial Aids, Devotional Life, Jesus Christ, the Church, the Bible, Commentaries on the Whole Bible and on particular books of the Bible, and Biography. I have discovered that once a minister remembers accurately just where books in a certain field are located in his study, and has placed in that particular section on his shelves a book which he knows deals with the particular subject because he has read it, he will be able to find it within a matter of a minute or two.

Someone will ask about the purchase of books. Books should not be purchased merely because they are books. I try to let two principles guide me in the purchase of books for my study: first, I am desirous of building up an adequate reference library. A busy minister hasn't time to run here and there and everywhere trying to find a book on a particular religious subject or in a specific religious field. He should possess in his own library at least one basic book in every field that he is called upon to know something about. This principle of selectivity will mean that the minister will be on the "lookout" for certain older, more standard works.

The second principle is this: a minister should purchase those new books which he believes will aid him in understanding the contemporary world and in preaching more effectively to the contemporary mind.

I am intensely interested in the contemporary world and therefore I must have certain periodicals coming to my desk. I want my denominational periodical. I want a magazine on missions. I need an ecumenical paper—one that sees the total Christian Church and surveys its task. Perhaps I need two ecumenical papers—each reflecting a different viewpoint; for after all, I need to know what is going on in the world of religion even if I don't agree with it all. And then perhaps I need a periodical aimed primarily at me as a preacher—to stimulate my mind, to encourage my spirit, to enlarge my faith, to inform me about pastoral techniques which have been found practical by other ministers. And, of course, I read one good secular daily newspaper. Let me recommend to you "The Christian Science Monitor." (You don't have to read the one religious editorial in each issue which is definitely sectarian.)

My mind is the analytical type of mind, and therefore I have many files. I realize some of the facetious things that have been said about files and filing systems: "Early Methodist preachers were going on to perfection; modern Methodist preachers are going on to systematization;" "a filing system is a systematic way of losing things." But I want to bear testimony to the fact that sensible filing systems, whose files are kept up-to-date, have been of inestimable value to me as a preacher. They have helped me keep "my imports ahead of my exports."

I use four filing systems for my resource materials: a clipping file, an illustration file, a quotation file, and a poetry file. I have adopted the following headings for my clipping file:

> Alcohol
> Amusements
> Apostles' Creed
> Archaeology
> Atheism
> Bible
> Bible - How to Study It
> Bible   Bible Characters

Bible   Old Testament - History
                         - Introduction
                         - Survey
                         - Individual Books

Bible - New   Testament - History
                         - Introduction
                         - Survey
                         - Individual Books

Biographical Sketches
Boy Scouts
Christianity and Other Religions

Christianity - Apologetics, Evidences
             - The Gospel
             - Christian Ethics
             - Christian Experience
               Christian Life
               Christian Sociology

Church
Church   Church Economics
          - Church Loyalty Crusades
          - Membership and Attendance
          - Planning Conferences

Church and State
Church and State - Communism
                   - Fascism
                   - Naziism
                   - Parochial Schools
                   - Shintoism

Church History - General Survey
                       - Early Christian Centuries
                       - Reformation - Martin Luther
                         Roman Catholic Church
                         Eastern Orthodox Churches
                         Christianity in England
                         Mysticism
                         Devotional Writings
                         Church Councils
                       - American Christianity
                             History
                       - American Christianity
                             Individual Protestant
                             Denominations

Christian Unity
Confucius
Cults
Devotional Materials
Evangelism
Friendship
Faith
Father
Gambling
God
Healing
Holy Spirit - Pentecost
Holy Spirit   Methodist Doctrine of Christian
                     Perfection
Immortality
Islam
Jesus Christ

Jesus Christ   Birth (Christmas)
                - Life
                - Disciples
                - Sermon on the Mount
                - Parables
                - Lent
                  Holy Week
                  Death
                  Resurrection (Easter)
                - Second Coming
Jew
Kingdom of God
Laymen
Life
Love
Methodism
Methodism - Relationship to Church of England
              - The Wesleys
                What Methodists Believe
                Francis Asbury
              - Methodists of the World
Minister - Life and Work
             Ministerial Aids
             Preaching
Missions
Modernism
Mother
Music
Negro
New Year
Oxford Group

Paul - Pauline Writings
Peter
Prayer
Racism
Red Cross
Religion - History of
Religion   Philosophy of
Religion and Education

Religion and Education - Church School
                                         - Teachers

Religion and the Home
Religion and Patriotism
Religion and Science
Religion and Sex
Salvation
Sin - Satan
Social Questions
Stewardship
Suffering   Trials
Sunday
Ten Commandments
Thanksgiving
Theology
United Nations
War and Peace
Woman
Work
Worship
Y. M. C. A.
Young People

As far as possible I use the same general headings for my other three files—illustrations, quotations, poetry. (I use 3x5 cards in these three files) Here are the topics in my illustration file, and with few exceptions, the same topics appear in the other two files:

Alcohol	Heredity
Amusements	Holy Spirit
Atheism	Home
Backsliding	Hope
Bible	Humility
Character	Immortality
Children	Individuality
Christ	Influence
Christian Experience	Judgment
Christian Life	Laughter
Christianity	Life
Church	Love
Consecration	Man
Courage	Missions
Criticism	Mother
Death	Music
Determination	Nation
Faith	Nature
Father	Negro
Friendship	Old Age
Christmas	Opportunity
God	Prayer
Gospel	Preaching
Happiness	Psalms
Heaven - Hell	Salvation

Science	Thoughts
Service	Time
Sin	Tolerance
Society	Trifles
Soul	Truth
Soul-Winning	Vicarious Suffering
Spiritual Awakening	Vision
Stewardship	War
Success	Woman
Suffering Trials	Wonder
Sunday	Work
Superstition	Worry
Temptation	Worship
Ten Commandments	Youth
Thanksgiving	

I likewise file my sermons according to a self-devised system. Each sermon is placed in an envelope and given a number. All sermons in the same series are given the same number, with consecutive letters after that number. I then classify the sermon and its particular code number in a handy notebook which contains the listing of all my sermons. However, in my Index of Sermons the listing is always made according to topic. In my Index I use different pages for listing sermons relating to each of the following topics:

Alcohol	Bible
Anniversary	Bible Characters
Apostles' Creed	Boy Scouts
Amusements	Children
Baccalaureate	Children's Day

Christian Life
Christmas
Church
Church Membership
    Church Loyalty
Church Finances
Commencement
Church School
Christian Unity
Deeper Life
Eschatology
Evangelism
Evangelistic Sermons
Father's Day
Funerals
Girl Scouts
Gospel
Healing
Holy Spirit
Home
Hymns
Immortality
Jesus Christ
  - Person
    Birth
  - Life
  - Miracles
  - Parables and Teaching
  - Lent
    Holy Week
    Death - Cross

- Seven Words from the
    Cross
- Resurrection
    Post-Resurrection
- Ascension
- Second Coming
Kingdom of God
Labor Day
Laymen
Methodism
Miscellaneous
Missions
Mother's Day
Music
Nature
New Year
Nation - Patriotism
Prayer
Prayer Meetings
Peace
Protestantism
Race
Radio Messages
Rural Life
Sacraments
Sanctification
Series of Sermons
Stewardship
Sunday School
Sunday
Satan

Thanksgiving	Women
Ten Commandments	Worship
War	Young Adults
Work	Young People

Because I keep my file of sermons up-to-date, it is with comparative ease and great efficiency that I can readily discover every sermon that I have in a specific area of Christian thought and life and every sermon in relation to the different days of the Christian year.

In addition to these permanent files, I also use two working files. One of these working files relates to the administrative activities of the church, to particular church programs and projects, and to those extra-church activities with which I am administratively associated. The other working file consists of "Sermon Suggestions." These may be sermon suggestions, in general, or relate to particular sermons already planned for use in the immediate future. It is amazing how much material relating to future sermons already planned for can be gathered by a preacher in the "ordinary line of duty and study" if he makes a master-plan of his preaching ahead of time.

The Minister and Preparing to Preach

The special burden of this series of lectures is not in the field of homiletics. Far be it from me to become so presumptuous as to suggest that I can tell others how to preach because I believe that I have mastered the art myself. However, no discussion of the continuing preparations of the minister would be complete unless we at least recognized the necessity of his continuing preparation in this matter of preaching.

I have a few basic convictions in this matter of preaching. I believe that it is generally true (of course, there are exceptions to every rule) that a minister succeeds or fails in direct proportion to the effectiveness or ineffectiveness of his preaching. I believe that preaching is more than a gift; it is also a discipline. And as a discipline I know that effective preaching demands continuing preparation. And I likewise know that when a minister ceases to make preparations for his preaching he ceases to "preach" in any vital, spiritual sense, even though he continues to be the minister of the church and to speak from the pulpit desk each Sunday.

There are innumerable factors which enter into a minister's preparation to preach. There are the preparation of himself, the preparation of his own spiritual experience, the preparation of his call to the ministry, the preparation of his formal education, the preparation of ministerial experience, and the preparation of detailed study in a particular field. When preparation in any of these areas, except that of formal schooling, is discontinued, the result is spiritually disastrous.

How does a minister prepare for his preaching assignments? What are the sources of sermon subjects? How does a person go about writing a sermon? As far as I am concerned, the sources of sermon topics are manifold. Among other sources I would list these: (1) what others have preached upon, particularly the preachers whose story is told in the Holy

Scriptures; (2) what a preacher knows and "feels" he ought to preach about; (3) suggestions which come from one's devotional reading; (4) what sincere people ask a minister to preach about; (5) preaching to meet the needs of the people, as the result of actual experiences. I think at once of a relevant illustration of this last-mentioned source of a sermon subject. I was visiting in a home where a young husband, thirty years of age, remarked to me: "I've never joined a church up to this time and so I suppose I never will." On my way home from that pastoral visit, I began thinking about "The Christ Who Breaks Old Patterns" and very soon I preached on that theme from my pulpit.

How does a man prepare a sermon? Here is my general procedure, and it has worked quite satisfactorily for me most of the time. Once I have chosen a particular subject or text upon which I feel I "must" preach, I immediately do two things: I start collecting the already-gathered source materials which I have in the field of the particular text or subject; and, secondly, I immediately give my sub-conscious mind an assignment by telling it over and over again that soon I must preach this sermon. It's wonderful what the sub-conscious mind will do for a preacher in the preparation of sermons, provided he has stored in it some related materials through the years, and provided it is free enough from negative and impeding influences so that it can function effectively. In this connection I am reminded of the following lines by Naoshi Koriyama, under the title "Soundless Work"—

"Green plants' process
Of photosynthesis
Is carried on silently
During the warm quiet day.
Yet the fruits
Of the soundless work
Are so eloquent:
The bulging corn and waving rice.

A poet's process
Of 'poemosynthesis'
Is carried on silently
During the moonless quiet night.
Yet the fruits
Of his quiet work
Are so eloquent:
An exquisite lyric and a glorious epic."
(*Quoted in "The Christian Science Monitor"*)

Then as the deadline for actual sermon preparation is reached, I engage in detailed and specific study on my sermon. And when I reach that "crucial" moment when the sermon begins to "break," as I call it, I undertake the work of outlining and developing it. Then comes the task of putting it all together—outline, exposition of the thoughts, illustrations, etc.—in a form that is not only worthy of presentation to the people but which is also "convenient to use" for the one who is to preach it.

Again let me remind you I am not intending to speak as one who has attained any homiletical "super-manhood." Rather, I am only meaning to suggest that the minister can never escape the imperative of making continuing preparations for his preaching.

THE DISCIPLINE OF THE SPIRIT

In our discussion of the continuing preparations of the minister from the perspective of The Disciplined Life we have spoken of the Discipline of the Self and the Discipline of the Mind. We hasten to speak of one further aspect of the Disciplined Life—the Discipline of the Spirit. When I speak of the minister's spirit I am not thinking primarily of his soul, as the seat of his spiritual life. We have already meditated upon the significance of the minister's soul when we considered the Discipline of the Self. Rather, do I think in terms of a minister's spirit as the manifestation of his soul, the outer expression of an inner quality of being, the minister's attitude and perspective, the effect that the minister's personality has upon others. The significance of the Disciplined Spirit cannot be over-estimated. Church people are quick to catch a minister's spirit and to be influenced and shaped thereby.

It appears to me that the minister's Discipline of his Spirit is in two directions—his attitude toward his calling, and his attitudes toward the people he serves. The minister's attitude toward his calling must ever be radiant, eager, creative, contemporary. To maintain such a spirit is not always easy, especially when the delusions of youth have faded and the grim realities of life confront on every hand. Illustrative of this is a very illuminating article which appeared recently in "The Methodist Recorder," under the title of "Half-Way House." "H. H." writes as follows:

They say that at forty a man becomes cynical. He has lived long enough to find out that the shining dreams of youth are not so easy to realize as once they seemed. They still call, but it is harder to pursue. The body is slower to respond, the mind burdened by the memory of past failures and present complexities. The temptation grows upon him to make light of his ideals and to pour contempt on his dreams.

It is not always realized by laymen how deadly is this danger to the minister approaching middle life. For twenty years he has preached the Gospel of God's renewing power. He has given himself to the shepherding of the flock and the routine tasks of the Church. In the beginning he set out, quick in body and mind, to turn the world upside down; but the world has proved heavier than he imagined.

The Methodist people . should also reserve a special place in their prayers for those who have spent their first strength, and may be feeling that they have spent it in vain.

But the minister has dreams that must never be forgotten. The dreams of youthful anticipation and of seminary days filled with unbridled eagerness must ever remain the fixed stars in the minister's horizon. What are some of these dreams of seminary days? "Everybody wants the Gospel;" "there is a brotherhood among Christian workers which is never marred by un-Christian attitudes and practices;" "honest and faithful work is quickly rewarded;" and "church work is always delightful and successful."—how glorious it is to dream! But, in spite of the sobering realities of life, in general, and of the ministry, in particular, the minister finds himself strangely guided by such dreams.

The minister must discipline his spirit in the acceptance of realities without the loss of ideals. He must become disciplined to the possible. A minister will never have his church just the way he wants it, for the church in a very real way is made by the voluntary response of a host of human wills. And if a preacher could get the church exactly the way he wants it, undoubtedly it would be so perfect that he no longer would be the kind of preacher that this perfect church would want.

The minister's spirit must become increasingly disciplined to the doing of a thing for the glory of it rather than for the glory of the results from the doing of it. It is the minister's true motive that disciplines his spirit triumphantly in his attitude toward his work. The minister's ideal is that expressed by the Psalmist: "I have set the Lord always before me." (Psalm 16:8.) The minister, like the disciples in the Scripture narrative of the first Palm Sunday, when asked, "Why are you doing this—with your life and your talents?" quickly answers: "The Lord hath need of it." The minister's motive is found in his whole-hearted consecration to Jesus Christ. The consecration of his mind: "one thing I know"—to know Christ; the consecration of his emotions: "one thing have I desired"—to love Christ; the consecration of his will: "one thing I do"— to obey Christ. It was Augustine Baker, who as a true minister of God, prayed: "My God, my desire is to serve Thee gratis, like a son, and not as a mercenary."

But the discipline of the minister's spirit also relates to his attitude toward the people he serves. His ministry, in every aspect and detail of it, must be performed in the spirit of love. The highest human compliment that can be paid to a minister is found in these words, "He just loved us." Love in the heart of the minister causes him to walk where his people walk and to share their burdens. It is such love in a minister's heart that enabled one to say of another, "He has your well-being very much at heart."

It is only a genuine love for others that will cause a minister to be personally interested in others and enable him to truly serve others. W. E. Sangster reminds us of this in these words:

> Missioners must learn the lesson no less than the missionaries. He who chooses to live in the slums that God may have his witness in areas which man has made vile, must settle with himself that his loving service of people must be utterly unconditional. He cannot love them in order that the people will cease to get drunk. He cannot love them in order that people will attend church. He cannot even love them in order that people will love God. He must love them for themselves alone, and go on loving them though they despise the gospel he preaches, impugn the motives which move him, and openly say that they discover some self-seeking purpose beneath all that he does. (**The Pure in Heart,** pp. 245, 246)

The minister ought to be the biggest-souled man in his congregation. And such big-soulness, created by love, will manifest itself in kindness. E. Stanley Jones aptly remarks: "If at the center of all our proofs of our being true ministers and workers for God is not kindness, then all the rest is sounding brass and tinkling cymbal." (*Growing Spiritually*, p. 174)

And the minister's love for his people must never be conditioned primarily by their love for him: there are many occasions when the minister will keep on loving in spite of—. How beautifully E. Stanley Jones has written again, words so full of spiritual meaning for us ministers:

"Don't go around with a chip on your shoulder, but with a Hand on your shoulder. Have a sense of mission, a sense of working out a plan, a Divine plan; and then you won't mind these hurts that come, for you are working out something big and important . . . Have a task so big that you'll not even feel the hurts along the way." (*Growing Spiritually*, p. 166)

The minister must be "all things to all men." He must undergo the discipline of being judged by all, yet judging no man. And his passion for his people must ever be akin to that of Paul: "And I will very gladly spend and be spent for you: though the more abundantly I love you, the less I be loved." (II Corinthians 12:15.)

How requisite is the discipline of the minister's spirit in the possession of abounding Christian love. David A. MacLennan has paraphrased the opening verses of I Corinthians 13 for a preacher in these lines:

Though I possess vast technical knowledge of sociology, psychology, political economy, so that I can speak correctly the impressive jargon of pundits in these fields, and have not the love which leads into creative personal contacts with people, I amount to nothing at all as a preacher of Christ. If I have that absolute faith and competence in dialectical theology so that I can confound the intellectuals and impress examiners of candidates for the highest academic degrees, but "couldn't care less" what my parishioners are up against in their families, their jobs, their leisure, and their inner lives, I should achieve precisely nothing in my preaching. (**Entrusted With The Gospel**)

Is there a secret that will guarantee the discipline of the minister's spirit? Yes, there is a spiritual secret. The secret of the minister's spirit is the Holy Spirit. Let the minister be filled with the Holy Spirit —let the Holy Spirit live in every part of the minister's being—then the beauty and grace and power of God's Spirit will flow out to others through the minister.

The disciplined Spirit, the disciplined Mind, the disciplined Self—these comprise the Disciplined Life for the minister. And only as the minister lives The Disciplined Life, under the guidance and influence of the Holy Spirit, does he engage in the continuing preparations so essential to his ministry. And only as he prepares and continues to prepare does he earn the right and keep the right to be a minister. For the Christian minister is "a workman that needeth not to be ashamed"—in his continuing preparations.

CHAPTER IV

NOT ASHAMED—IN HIS CARE OF THE CHURCH

"Beside those things that are without, that which cometh upon me daily, the care of all the churches."
II Corinthians 11:28

The moment you speak of a pastor, you must also think in terms of a parish; and when you talk of a minister, you must reckon with the people to be ministered to. And at the center of our Christian conception of a parish there is the institution of the local church. The people to be ministered to are those related, in any way, to a particular local church; and the constituency of a parish is defined in terms of the outreach of a specific church.

Thus, the pastor finds himself, first of all, related to an institution, an organization, which is known as a local church, and of which he is either the appointed or elected leader. And "the care" of that church becomes the dominant responsibility of the minister. In our day, an age that is highly organized and institutionalized, and in which the structure of the church reflects this organization and institutionalization so evident in the world outside the church, the matter of a minister's administration of a church is of tremendous importance, for the minister is called upon to be the leader of an "institution," and, as the servant of God in this capacity he must be "a workman that needeth not to be ashamed."

At the very outset of our discussion of the minister's "care" of the church, we must affirm that the minister who expects to succeed in the administration of a church must possess the basic characteristics of an effective leader. The qualities of leadership must be resident in the Christian minister. Let us take a hasty glance at this matter of leadership. What is it? What qualities of life characterize it? How is true leadership manifest?

Morten Ten Hoor, a contemporary American educator, tells us that: "the safe leader is one who understands his place in the world and can thus envisage the place of his fellow men; who can morally respect himself and can thus be respected by others; who has learned to control his emotions and can thus be trusted to exert control over others; who has learned to live in peace and contentment with himself and can thus with propriety urge others to do likewise."

In an article entitled "What Makes Executives Tick?", the content of which was arrived at factually, Roy Rutherford, who says of himself, "My job is studying men—and executives are my specialty," concludes that there are at least eighteen characteristics of effective leadership. Here is Mr. Rutherford's formidable list:

1. Leaders work hard
2. Leaders have imagination
3. Leaders believe in research
4. Leaders have good memories
5. Leaders have determination
6. Leaders are modest

7. Leaders are timesavers
8. Leaders are ambitious
9. Leaders know human nature
10. Leaders are self-confident
11. Leaders listen well
12. Leaders get along with people
13. Leaders are frank
14. Leaders are articulate
15. Leaders are family men
16. Leaders are educated
17. Leaders are good sports
18. Leaders are sincere

(Quoted in *The Rotarian*)

Here is "A Prescription for Leadership" suggested by Harold C. Kessinger, an educator:

The ideal leader has vision without being a visionary.
He can listen reflectively.
He can think creatively.
He can talk inspiringly.
He can work cooperatively.
He is courteous without being vacillating.
He is courageous without being dominating.
He knows how to delegate duties without avoiding his own.
He always shares recognition and rewards with others.
He has enthusiastic co-workers rather than sheep-like followers.
He knows the shortest path, but will take the longer way if he can attain the same objective with less friction.
He knows how to compromise in non-essentials without sacrificing fundamentals. (Quoted in **The Rotarian**)

Most people, with a few political exceptions, agree that President Dwight D. Eisenhower manifests the qualities of effective leadership. After he was first elected President of the U. S. A., I chanced to read an article entitled "How Eisenhower Works—He'll Be a Different Kind of President." The author gave nine characteristics of Mr. Eisenhower, as a leader, and I have been impressed that these characteristics will be found in all true leadership:

1. He plans
2. He organizes the work load
3. He consults
4. He delegates
5. He avoids friction
6. He decides
7. He avoids overwork
8. He speaks carefully
9. He keeps power

(Quoted in **U. S. News and World Report**)

Recently two industrial psychologists, employed by George Fry and Associates, management consultants, subjected thirty-three top Chicago executives to an exhaustive series of tests and questions in order to answer the question, "What's the top-level executive like and how did he get that way?" The answers are revelatory. Above average intellectual ability seems to be a requisite for leadership. The executive tends to be on the serious side. He is a warm and spontaneous fellow who usually creates a good first impression and maintains friendship easily. Leaders are usually positive and decisive individuals. They are just average in emotional stability. They are often motivated to success by a need for accomplishment and a fear of failure. Their main interest is in dealing with people. Most of the executives interviewed were raised in homes with good personal relations. They were well educated, with an average college grade of "B"—hence they were good but not exceptional students. A majority of the leaders stated that skill in human relations was most important in their own advancement.

Is it not clearly evident that there is a radical difference between a boss and a leader? The boss drives his men; the leader coaches them. The boss depends on authority; the leader, on good will. The boss inspires fear; the leader inspires enthusiasm. The boss says, "I"; the leader says, "We." The boss assigns his tasks; the leader sets the pace. The boss says, "Get here on time!"; the leader gets there ahead of time. The boss fixes the blame for the breakdown; the leader fixes the breakdown. The boss knows how it is done; the leader shows how. The boss makes work a drudgery; the leader makes it a game. The boss says, "Go!"; the leader says, "Let's go!"

Charles M. Schwab once said: "I have never had a man work for me; I have had thousands work with me."

As the Christian minister seeks to manifest and develop the high qualities of leadership he must remember that there is a personal price to be paid for effective leadership. In his translation J. B. Phillips has the Apostle John in his third Epistle say of Diotrephes that although he wants to be leader he refuses to perform the duties of such leadership. And what is the personal price of such leadership? The Christian minister must consecrate his natural endowments of mind and body to the service of Jesus Christ. Under the influence of the Holy Spirit he must continually develop his abilities and skills in leadership.

And constantly he must use the power inherent in such personal leadership for the glory of God and for the good of his fellows.

We move on to consider the question—"What is involved, on the part of the minister, in the administration of a church?" I would answer, in the first place, that the minister, as administrative leader, must have an adequate ideal for the church's life and activity. Basic in the discovery of such an ideal for a local church is one's understanding of the Scripture idea and ideal of the church. No more adequate doctrine of the church has been formulated than that given us by the Apostle Paul in his epistles. Paul's first great service to the Early Christian Church was in supplying it with a philosophy of existence. He saw with sure insight into its essential nature. He gave a definition of the church which is valid in every age, for it lays hold of what is common to a true church, whenever and wherever it is formed. Paul's doctrine is that a genuine church is "the body of Christ." (Ephesians 4:12; Romans 12:4, 5; I Corinthians 12:12-26; Colossians 1:18; 3:14, 15.) Paul is telling us that a church is a social organism in which Christ's Spirit prevails.

The word "body," or organism, as applied to the church is a very suggestive figure of speech. Bishop F. Gerald Ensley lists the following eleven characteristics of a physical body which apply spiritually to a church:

1. A body is a living unity-in-diversity.
2. A body is a "fellowship" of its component parts.

3. A body is a servant to the spirit.
4. A body requires a basic structure, a skeleton, to achieve its end.
5. A body is a whole of interdependent parts.
6. A body is so put together that what hurts one organ hurts all.
7. There come times when the body must sacrifice one of its organs for the health of the whole.
8. A body is a union of change and identity.
9. A body lives by appropriating what is not itself and transforming it into its own nature.
10. A body has an amazing power of self-maintenance.
11. Life comes only from life.

(Paul's Letters to Local Churches)

In the light of the Scripture ideal of the church as "the body of Christ," as "the bride of Christ," I, as administrative leader of a local church, must determine and keep constantly in mind what kind of church I want my church to become, what kind of results I want my church to witness during my ministry. In my opinion, no finer ideal for a church has ever been offered than that found in these words—"Let the Church be the Church." Let it be the church—the church patterned in its aims and spirit after the Early Church, but ministering effectively to people in the particular age in which it serves.

There is a second general remark that I would make: the minister must have an understanding of and a deep conviction concerning the place of the minister as the administrative leader of a church. It appears to be basic in the Protestant conception of the Christian ministry that the pastor is the leader of a church. This is not to depreciate in any way the significant place of laymen in the local church. Rather, it is to spell out the relationship between minister and laymen in the administration of a church. Paul tells us that the minister is a master-builder. (I Corinthians 3:10.) We are reminded of some words of Dr. Charles E. Jefferson, about the minister's objective: "Let everything be done with a view to building!" The minister builds upon the foundation of Jesus Christ. Others labor with the minister in the building. Cephas, Apollos, Epaphroditus, Philemon, Barnabas, Luke, Epaphras were not competitors—they were cooperators. And in "building" the congregation is exhorted to follow the spiritual leader—"Be ye followers of me, even as I also am of Christ." (I Corinthians 11:1.)

In the third place, the minister must have a realistic approach to his administrative situation. He must make a personal diagnosis and evaluation of his particular church and seek to discover just what is the relationship between the actual situation as he finds it and the "ideal" for the church toward which he aspires. I have always been impressed by the fact that when Jesus entered Jerusalem on that first Palm Sunday He went into the Temple and looked around first. His diagnosis of the situation preceded and determined the course of his subsequent action, which resulted in the driving out of the money-changers from God's House.

How realistic the Apostle Paul was in his pastoral

relation to the church at Corinth. Well he knew that there were at least the following major problems in that church: (1) factions; (2) immorality; (3) litigation between Christians; (4) questions concerning marriage and divorce; (5) over-conscientiousness; (6) the veiling of women; (7) misbehavior at the Lord's Supper; (8) the use and abuse of spiritual gifts; (9) questions concerning the resurrection of the body; (10) disputes over spiritual authority in the church. It was in the light of these things that Paul realistically sought to lead the church at Corinth in the direction of more Christian conduct and activity.

Such a realistic diagnosis of his own church will remain, for the most part, the minister's private property. Conscientiously he will use what has been discovered by it only at the proper time and for the common good.

Thus it logically follows that the minister as administrative leader must be able to adjust the actual, the realistic, to the ideal, the objective. On the basis of his diagnosis of the needs of his church, the minister must work out a master plan and program for his ministry of a particular church, and also detailed, related plans for specific aspects of his ministry. At all times, in the administration of a church, a minister must know just where he is going. He must never be like the preacher who lost his brief case in which were kept his appointment book and his sermons. The tragedy of it all was this: that preacher didn't know where he was going nor what he was going to say when he got there.

And just as apropos to our discussion at this point is the story of the hitchhiker who was picked up by a tourist and at the end of the ride was offered a newspaper to take along with him. He thanked the driver and added, "I'll take it home to Momma to read to me." Astonished, the driver asked, "Can't you read, my friend?" "Well," said the hitchhiker, "by the time I left school I had only learned to read figures, not letters." "Oh," remarked his friend, "I guess in our day of big business it's more important to know how to read figures than letters." To which the hitchhiker immediately replied, "But it's awfully inconvenient for a hitchhiker; for when you come to a roadsign you can find out HOW FER but not WHERE TO." Seriously speaking, the minister must always know "where to" in his administration of a church.

In the light of his situation, under the influence of the Scripture Ideal of the church, and guided by the Holy Spirit, the minister must arrange his church program in general and work out all related programs. The Holy Spirit must be the administrator of the minister as he decides his course as the administrative leader of the church. How beautifully expressive are the words found in I Chronicles 28:12—"the pattern of all that he had by the Spirit."

I continue with a fifth suggestion. The minister should have a correct understanding of and make full and proper use of the organizational structure provided by one's denomination for the purpose of making the local church more efficient in its administration and more effective in its work. Take, for illustration, the organizational structure provided for the local church by The Methodist Church (U.S.A.). Each local church has a Board of Trustees; an Official Board (which includes the stewards); four commissions—Education, Membership and Evangelism, Missions, Stewardship and Finance; certain specified Quarterly Conference committees; and such Official Board committees as are needed. This structure of the local church has been provided by the denomination on the basis of study and experience, and all the possibilities of such an organizational setup should be used to the full. It is never logical or truthful to say that "this or that" piece of organizational machinery will not work, until it has been given a fair trial. All other things being equal, a local church organized in the manner prescribed by its denomination has a greater chance of being effective than one which is not organized or poorly organized. Do not misunderstand me—organization is not synonymous with success. But organization often provides a clear channel through which the power of the Spirit of God flows if invited to do so.

Furthermore, the minister must guard jealously the purpose of his personal relationship to each administrative group within the church. While it is true that he must be related personally to each administrative group and maintain a working relationship to each, yet he is never to presume to take the place of any such administrative group, nor to become the "slave" of any such group in the doing of its assigned tasks. Rather, the minister's task is to counsel with each group, and to encourage each group in the effective accomplishment of its work, and to see to it that the total program of the church, as carried out through the various groups, is a unified program. After all, the minister is the only person in the administrative life of the church who sees the church's program in its totality. His responsibility is to make sure that the program and work of each group within the church contributes to the larger objective and long-range perspective of the total church.

And so, in reality, the minister finds himself the leader of a "team," a team of devoted individuals, a team of efficient organizations, who are working with one grand objective: to make the "actual" within the church approximate more fully the Divine Ideal for the church as "the body of Christ."

A seventh suggestion needs to be offered. The minister as spiritual leader of the church, must see to it that the total administrative program of the church is undergirded with prayer. After all, the church is basically a spiritual organism, engaged in a spiritual warfare, and dependent upon spiritual weapons and powers for the accomplishment of its ends. How true it is that "we wrestle not against flesh and blood, but against principalities, against powers, against the rulers of the darkness of this world, against spiritual wickedness in high places." (Ephesians 6:12.) "The race is not to the swift, nor the battle to the strong." (Ecclesiastes 9:11.) For, as God says, speaking through the prophet Zechariah: "Not by might, nor by power, but by My Spirit, saith the Lord of hosts." (4:6) The "wise man" of the Book of Proverbs reminds us that "many are the plans in the mind of a man, but it is the purpose of the Lord that will be established." (Proverbs 19:21, R.S.V.)

The total program of the church, and the specific programs of the church, must be undergirded by prayer. There should be held general prayer meetings for the life of the church and its total program. There should, likewise, upon occasion be held special prayer services on behalf of particular projected programs of the church. As I wrote these lines my church was engaged in a large Fund-Raising Campaign for needed additions and renovations to our church property. On the opening Sunday night of the crusade, I appealed to my people to engage in believing prayer in behalf of this significant program—personal prayer, prayer at the family altar, public prayer at church meetings, and at meetings of each organization.

Still speaking in general terms, I make an eighth and final suggestion about the minister as the administrative head of the local church. At all times, and in every administrative circumstance, the minister must be a man of steady vision, of steadfast purpose, and at the same time a person of unusual patience and unwavering perseverance. A minister's wisest and most carefully worked out "dreams" for his church will never be realized overnight. They must be worked out, step by step, stage by stage, and often only after discouraging and serious setbacks.

Many, many times the minister will find himself literally "hemmed in" because of the attitudes and opposition of some of the people with whom he is compelled to work. The minister's leadership is often with people who are not easily led. These realistic words of Simeon Stylites are readily understood by a minister:

> The pastor of St. John's-by-the-Gas-Station was whistling merrily as he walked down the street. I recognized a familiar tune from the Mikado, "I've Got a Little List." I said to him, "I recognize from your disturbance of the atmosphere that you have a little list." "That I have," he replied gleefully. "I've got a little list of people in a church who are an irritant to every pastor. In fact, they are usually pests. I do not advocate calling in a pest exterminator, but they should be identified and at least included in the litany, 'Good Lord, deliver us!'" (Quoted in **The Christian Century**)

And in such times, dealing with such people, the minister will be tempted to a most aggravated form of impatience. One is reminded of something that "Dig or Die," Brother Hyde, wrote in his autobiography: "I went to my room. And to my knees. 'God, put a bit in my mouth and hold me back when I want to take the reins and run. Keep me from the sin of impatience.'"

The minister must remember constantly that his gracious tact and loving patience in dealing with those who become temptations to impatience, become the shining credential of his continuing right to leadership in his church. Yes, if a minister hopes to succeed as administrative leader, he must be a man of steady vision, of enduring patience, of expanding love, of realistic optimism, of great grace!

Now, before discussing three specific administrative strategies that have been of great help to me, permit me to state what I believe should be the transcendent principle, humanly speaking, of a minister's ad-

ministrative life. Here is the principle succintly stated:
the minister, as administrative head, must remain objective in his leadership of the church. While he must
be utterly subjective in his relationship to the Christ
of the church—obeying the Divine Will implicitly—in
relationship to his working administratively with
church people, he must remain objective. He is not
partisan, nor a leader of factions. He is not out to see
a certain clique in the church dominate everything and
everybody. Rather, he is the leader, the administrator,
of the church, and keeping his eye upon Jesus Christ
"the author and finisher of his faith" he must keep his
administrative ideal high and worthy at all times. And
what worthier administrative ideal could a minister
have than that professed by the great Apostle himself:
"For I determined not to know anything among you,
save Jesus Christ, and Him crucified." (I Corinthians
2:2)

The first administrative technique that has been
of great practical aid to me in the administration of a
church is the holding of an organizational dinner meeting at the beginning of each church year. All members
of the Official Board and of the commissions and committees of the church are invited to this meeting. It
has usually been held on a Saturday evening. The
meeting begins with a fellowship dinner, served at a
nominal cost. The chairman of the Official Board presides at the dinner and speaks briefly to the group
about the importance of all administrative assignments
in the life of the church.

The schedule immediately following the dinner

consists of a series of consecutive meetings of the different commissions and committees of the church. The meeting of each commission and committee is for one purpose only: to organize the group by electing officers for the new church year. The minister presides at each group meeting, and the time of each meeting never exceeds ten minutes. This makes it possible for all the commissions and committees to meet during one evening.

The values of such an annual organizational meeting are threefold: (1) at the beginning of the new church year each member of a commission or committee is fully informed of his particular administrative assignment for the year; (2) each commission and committee by being fully organized at the very beginning of the year is ready for all necessary activity whenever the occasion arises; and (3) the early organization of all administrative groups makes possible the publication of an official church directory for use during the year.

A second administrative strategy which I recommend wholeheartedly is the holding of an annual Planning Conference for the new church year. Methodists will be interested in learning that the 1956 General Conference adopted legislation calling upon every official board to hold an annual Planning Conference. Just what is a Planning Conference? A Planning Conference is a meeting of interested and responsible persons within a church for the purpose of outlining definite objectives and programs for a local church and its departments during a particular church year.

It has been my experience that the constituency of a Planning Conference may be comprised of any of four different groups of people: (1) the total membership of a church may be invited (this is practical only in a small church); (2) or the Planning Conference may be attended by all the administrative officials of a church—the Board of Trustees, the Official Board, the members of the commissions and the committees; (3) or it may be limited to the members of the Official Board; (4) or the active participants in such a conference may be limited to the minister and selected leaders of the various areas of the church's life and activity.

There are three main types of Planning Conferences: (1) those purely administrative in purpose aimed at the church's program; (2) those primarily spiritual in nature aimed at the spiritual lives of those attending; (3) those which combine the consideration of administrative details with a spiritual discipline for those attending.

Let us suppose that the annual planning conference is of the first type—primarily administrative in its purpose. Such a Planning Conference should be divided into three sections: Retrospect, Prospect, Dedication.

Retrospect: Each member of the Planning Conference should be faced with such questions as these:

(1)   What do you consider to have been the outstanding accomplishment of our church during the past year?

(2) What do you consider to have been the outstanding weaknesses of our church during the past year?

The members, meeting as organizational groups, should consider these questions:

(1) What is the general purpose of this organizational group as it relates to the total church program?

(2) What are the accomplishments of this organizational group during the past year?

(3) What have been the weaknesses of this organizational group during the past year?

Prospect: Each individual member of the Planning Conference will attempt to answer these questions:

(1) What do you think ought to be changed in our church program and procedure?

(2) What goals in the various fields of church activity should our church set for the new church year?

(3) What do you think should be the primary goal of our church during this new church year?

Each organizational group at a Planning Conference is asked to report to the whole group on the following:

(1) What are the specific objectives of this organizational group for the new church year?

(2) How will these aims and goals be realized during the new church year?

(3) Are there any suggestions that will help increase the effectiveness of our church?

Of course, all of the evaluating suggestions of individual members and of organizational groups at a Planning Conference are screened by a carefully selected committee and the findings reported to the entire constituency of the Planning Conference for discussion and decision. (Needless to say, an effective Planning Conference cannot be held in thirty minutes or an hour. A minimum time of an afternoon and an evening is required.) Before the conference is ended, the total group, under wise leadership, is able to arrive at a commendable program of objectives and activities for the new church year, which program will be reported to the various administrative groups within the church for action.

Dedication: Before the Planning Conference adjourns there must be afforded an opportunity for dedication. With the new church year ahead, and with some well-defined goals in view, each administrative leader within the church's life must dedicate himself anew to Jesus Christ for a new anointing of God's Spirit for the tasks lying immediately ahead.

Now let us suppose that the annual Planning Conference is in the nature of a spiritual retreat. Then each member must undergo a personal spiritual "checkup." How rewarding a spiritual experience it would be if each official member, if each member of a church, would ask himself such questions as these:

Am I a man of the strictest honesty?

Do I speak the truth?

Do I pay my debts?

Am I known as a Christian where I work?

Are some people outside the Church because I am inside?

What am I like at home?

Do those who know me best believe in me most?

Do I criticize the Church and other Christians in front of the children?—heedless or careless that it is nearly the most damning thing I could do for them?

Do I acknowledge God (guests or no guests) with grace before meals; and do I ever call the family to prayer?

Do I mount a constant guard on my tongue? or is my heart so full of God that even my most unpremeditated words could only be of love?

Am I critical of others?

Is it possible that I claim to be a Christian and nurse revenge?

Do I live day by day in conscious dependence on God and alert to the guidance of Heaven?

Do I find time early in every day for Bible study, unhurried prayer, quiet listening to God?

Do I love God's Day, His Word, His holy Table?

Do I love to go to God's House?

Can I work with other people? And can other people work with me?

Do I want God's cause to advance, or is it my chief desire that I should advance it?

Am I willing to take my wages in Christian service from God alone?

How much money do I give God?

What about tithing?

Does the Holy Spirit dwell in me?
Can I love the people I don't like?
Am I a happy Christian?
Am I temperate in all things?
How much of my life is really given to others?
Is my love real enough to show itself in service?
(Sangster, W. E., *A Spiritual Check-up*)

If the annual Planning Conference is in the nature of a spiritual retreat for an official group representing the church, then a "spiritual check-up" for the church must be engaged in. I recommend another of Dr. Sangster's pamphlets, *A Check-up for Our Church,* as an excellent guide for such spiritual discipline. Dr. Sangster would have each official church group consider the following spiritual questions:

1. What is the church for?
2. Is our church a center of reverent worship?
3. What quality of life does our church produce?
4. What is our church doing for the children?
5. What is our church doing for youth?
6. What is our church doing for women?
7. What is our church doing for men?
8. What is our church doing for those who never attend?
9. What is our church doing for the afflicted and fallen?
10. What is our church doing to fight social evils?
11. What is our church doing for the wider world?

If the purpose of an annual Planning Conference includes both the administrative and spiritual emphases then, of course, a carefully arranged program including both emphases must be worked out. If such a conference were an afternoon and evening affair, perhaps the afternoon session could be devoted to the spiritual and the evening to the administrative.

As a minister I can testify to the fact that the conducting of regular and well-arranged Planning Conferences each church year is of inestimable value both to the personal spiritual lives of those who attend and to the administrative life of the total church.

A third administrative strategy which I recommend heartily is the establishment of a Minister's Cabinet. As minister, I have formed into a cabinet, for purposes of counsel and guidance administratively, the heads of the various areas of administrative activity in the church. For illustration, in my present church, the following church leaders are members of the cabinet: assistant minister (who is also Director of Youth) chairman of the Official Board, president of the Board of Trustees, Church Lay Leader, the chairman of the four commissions (Education, Membership and Evangelism, Missions, Stewardship and Finance), president of the Woman's Society of Christian Service, president of the Ushers' Association, leader of Young Adults, leader of Intermediate Youth, and the chairman of the Music Committee.

The Minister's Cabinet meets monthly, and upon special call. The cabinet has no legislative or executive standing in the church structure. Its function is purely advisory and recommendatory. The meeting of the cabinet provides a wonderful opportunity just for talking things over as they relate to the total life of the church. The whole philosophy of the church's existence is evaluated. A cabinet meeting becomes the occasion to hear and discuss criticisms which have been levelled at the church. Weaknesses of the church's program are frankly faced. Suggested modes of procedure for this or that department of the church are scrutinized thoroughly. The schedule of events for a church year is carefully considered. And the result of it all is that from month to month the Minister's Cabinet makes valid recommendations for future action to the various administrative groups in the church. And may I add that many of the most progressive things that have happened during my ministry in my present and my former churches had their inception in meetings of the Minister's Cabinet. I would urge strongly that every minister, early in his experience as administrator of a local church, at least give this idea of the organization of a Minister's Cabinet a fair trial. I believe it will pay big dividends administratively.

I am the first person to recognize and admit that in this discussion of the administrative leadership of the minister I have spoken in the most general of terms and have omitted any discussion of most of the specific administrative areas of a church's life. Within the church the minister is the administrative leader of the educational work, of youth work, of stewardship and finance, of benevolence and missions, of evangelism, and of men's and women's work. Likewise, he must manifest leadership in his personal relations —with his staff, with those engaged in the ministry of music, with the ushers, with the official board and

with the various commissions and committees. And
then there are the areas of leadership outside the local
church—in the field of public relations, with the press
and radio, and with the public in general; in the area
of the community, with the varied related civic en-
terprises; and in the realm of inter-church relations,
with the various evangelical church groups who are
often called upon to work together on common ventures
of faith and social righteousness. Truly each of these
specific areas of ministerial leadership demands individual and detailed study, but the limits of our discussion make such prohibitive. Perhaps the guiding
principles of church administration that we have been
considering will aid each of us in working out administrative procedures when we find ourselves confronted by specific demands.

In fairness, however, to the total picture of church
administration, I must mention briefly two imperatives
which devolve upon a minister. First, the minister, as
the leader of the church, is responsible for the development of lay leadership within the church membership.
Too often both ministers and laymen have thought
that ministers were the only leaders in the church.
This is a fatal fallacy, and wherever it is acted upon
and followed, only disheartening consequences in the
life of the church have resulted.

The church consists of both ministers and laymen;
each of whom has a distinctive administrative function
to perform in the church, and neither of whom can
attempt to do the work of the other without distinct
loss to the church itself. The minister is responsible

for both the discovery and development of lay leadership within the church. Perhaps Elton Trueblood has overstated the case, but the principle is valid, when he writes:

"The good minister is not one who desires to be the whole show or the center of attention. He desires rather to be a catalytic agent, stirring up lay members to activity and perfectly satisfied if his contribution is not seen or known. The best minister makes himself progressively unnecessary." (*Signs of Hope*, p. 86)

Jesus called and trained and used laymen. Is there not a symbolical action on His part, revealed in a study of His miraculous feeding of the multitude, when He gave the loaves to His disciples and the disciples gave them to the multitudes? (Matthew 14:19.) Let us always remember that the first disciples and the early apostles were laymen. The training of the Twelve was, in reality, the development of lay leadership.

St. Paul recognized the place of lay personnel in the work of the church. Hear him as he wrote to Timothy: "And the things that thou hast heard of me among many witnesses, the same commit thou to faithful men, who shall be able to teach others also." (II Timothy 2:2.)

In the church today lay people need to be trained for every area of leadership in the church: administrative leadership, educational leadership, evangelistic and missionary leadership, stewardship leadership, spiritual leadership.

But the important question is, "How can such necessary lay leadership be raised up?" I answer only in the most general terms, giving five bits of practical counsel to ministers. First, the minister must realize the absolute necessity of adequate lay leadership in the local church. The task of the local church is entirely too big to be performed apart from it. On the other hand, it is surprising how much can be done when nobody, and this includes the minister, cares who gets the credit for the doing of it.

Second, potential leadership must be discovered among the membership of the church. Many methods attempting to discover leadership abilities are utilized by churches. In my present church we use a Stewardship Survey card. We keep on file a record of every member's stewardship interests and abilities. Here is a copy of the actual card we use:

We have worked out a list of nearly one hundred activities within the life of our church. Each activity is codified by a number, and under the proper topical heading—such as men's work, women's work, youth work, etc.—the number of the particular activity is placed on the member's card. Then an accurate and up-to-date classification of the total membership, in relation to their abilities and interests, is made available to the different groups within the church.

Once we have discovered leadership ability in an individual, we must enlist him in the use of it, on behalf of his church. We must challenge him by convincing him that we sincerely believe in the potential of leadership that is within him. It is amazing what big things we get from a person when we expect big things of him. And, furthermore, we must challenge

LOCAL CHURCH MEMBERSHIP STATUS
CONSTITUENCY - STEWARDSHIP RECORD

Church	Nursery Roll	Nursery 2-3	Kinder-garten 4-5	Primary 6-8	Junior 9-11	Inter-mediate 12-14	Youth 15-23	Young Adult 24-34	Adult

First Name _____ Initial _____ Last Name _____

Address _____ Street _____ City (if other than local) _____

Birthday _____ Month _____ Day _____ Telephone _____

Family Name (if other than listed above) _____ Occupation _____

Date _____ Recorded by _____

FAMILY RELATIONSHIP

Head of Family	Wife	Son	Daughter	Father	Mother	Other (State)

STEWARDSHIP INTERESTS

Men's Work	Women's Work	Youth Work	Visitation	Educa-tion	Missions	Finance	Music	Office Work	Publicity	Food Service	Visual Aids

Decora-tions	Church Nursery	Ushering	Recrea-tion	Crafts	Other Interests

FILE INDEX _____

him with the tremendous demand for the Christian stewardship of such leadership ability.

In the fourth place, we must train those we have judged to be capable of leadership. Such training should be not only in the general field of leadership but in the specific fields of church activity, such as church administration, church finance, evangelism, education, missions, and the like.

Finally, these trained leaders must be used as leaders. Not just trained for leadership—but actually placed in positions of leadership. Here again it is true that experience is the best teacher. What a tremendous difference would be manifest in the "production story" of the average church if there could be discovered and trained and used real leaders from within its own membership.

A further imperative which challenges the minister as the administrative head of the church is his responsibility to take the lead in the recruitment of young people for full-time Christian service. Such a statement is not meant to depreciate in any way the significance of the Christian doctrine of vocation. Every Christian's life and work must be viewed as the calling of God. But in addition to Christian-life service there must also be Christian Life-Service. Young men and women must be recruited for full-time Christian service.

This is particularly true in relation to the Christian ministry. A recent survey conducted by The Methodist Church reveals that 1600 new preachers are needed annually for this denomination. And the local minister, both because of his position and influence, has a strategic responsibility in the recruitment of young men for the Christian ministry. The influence of the minister in recruiting young men for the ministry is revealed by another recent study which shows that 34% of the young ministers surveyed were influenced, primarily from a human standpoint, by their ministers in answering the call to preach. This is unusually significant in view of the fact that only 17.4% gave their mothers and only 11.2% listed their fathers as the chief human influence.

How can the local pastor fulfil his responsibility in this matter of recruitment? Here again I shall speak only in general terms. Each minister naturally will develop his own technique. The minister must constantly emphasize the spiritual aspects of the total work of the church. It is in such a spiritual atmosphere that the call of God to young lives is most frequently heard. The minister, by the example of his own ministry, must reveal to youth the glory of "the high calling of God."

The minister must always be a friend to youth. He must use youth in the program of the church on every possible occasion. He must be known at all times as one upon whom the youth can call and with whom they may freely and confidently counsel, and particularly in matters that relate to personal spiritual living and to God's will for one's life. And, of course, there must be particular occasions when the minister gives the youth of his church a definite opportunity for making a Life Commitment to full-time Christian service. Oh, how blessed are the satisfactions of a minister who can look back upon a ministry in which there were not only erected temples of wood and brick and stone, but in which there were also raised up "spiritual sons" in the ministry!

As we conclude we think again of the words of the Apostle Paul, with which we began—"Beside those things that are without, that which cometh upon me daily, the care of all the churches." The minister must be "a workman that needeth not to be ashamed" in his care of the church.

But, in the light of all the sobering responsibilities of church administration, men across the centuries have asked and will continue to ask: "Who is sufficient for these things?"—"Just what kind of man does it take to be the pastor of a church?" How true are the words spoken to a young preacher, in a recent novel: "You are a pastor now, brother, and a pastor needs the tact of a diplomat, the strength of Samson, the patience of Job, the wisdom of Solomon—and a cast-iron stomach." (James Street, *The Gauntlet*)

I think we can understand what a native Chinese preacher meant when he addressed a large conference of Christian workers in these words:

Ask the Lord Jesus for Peter's hook to bring up fish, David's crook to guide the sheep aright, Gideon's torch to light up the dark places, Moses' guiding rod, David's sling to prostrate your giant foe, the brazen serpent to cure the bites of the world's snakes, gospel seed with no tares in it, and above all, the wonderful Holy Spirit to help at all times.

"Who is sufficient for all these things?" Only the minister who is totally dedicated to Jesus Christ and who is filled with the Holy Spirit. The late Bishop Thomas Ken expressed it beautifully:

> Give me the Priest these graces shall possess—
> Of an ambassador the just address:
> A father's tenderness, a shepherd's care,
> A leader's courage, which the Cross can bear;
> A ruler's awe, a watchman's wakeful eye,
> A pilot's skill, the helm in storm to ply;
> A fisher's patience, and a laborer's toil,
> A guide's dexterity to disembroil,
> A prophet's inspiration from above,
> A teacher's knowledge, and a saviour's love.
>
> Who is all that he would others be,
> From wilful sin, though not from frailty free,
> Who still keeps Jesus in his heart and head,
> Who strives in steps of our Arch-Priest to tread,
> Who can himself and all the world deny,
> Lives pilgrim here, but denizen on high.

Truly every good minister of Jesus Christ as he assumes the leadership of a church voices in his own heart these prayerful words, penned by Grace Noll Crowell:

> Lord God of all the churches of all lands,
> Thou hast given me this church in which to serve
> As Thy Assistant. I would be Thy hands,
> Thy steadfast heart, Thy feet.—I would not swerve
> From the clearly outlined course that Thou hast laid
> For the Shepherds of Thy people. Be my Guide,
> Ground me so firmly, may I be so stayed
> That I can ably meet the trust implied.

I will be selfless, Lord, at this Thy task,
I would be willing to be sacrificed
That I may do the one thing Thou dost ask:
To glorify Thy Son, the living Christ.
I would be fearless, Lord, at any cost,
I would be understanding, faithful, true,
Lord God, whatever earthly prize be lost,
Help me to do what Thou wouldst have me do.

CHAPTER V

NOT ASHAMED—IN HIS SPIRITUAL LEADERSHIP OF HIS PEOPLE

"Be ye followers of me, even as I also am of Christ."
I Corinthians 11:1

When we speak of the spiritual leadership of the Christian Minister we are face-to-face with the spiritual idea and ideal which are basic in the concept of THE PASTOR. The Christian Minister is called to be a pastor, a shepherd of souls. Charles E. Jefferson, that mighty pastor of a past generation, continues to speak to us today in these challenging words:

Of all the titles which have been minted for the envoys of the Son of God, that of "Shepherd" is the most popular, the most beautiful, and the most ample.

If, then, we are the successors of the apostles, we must have the apostolic spirit and do the apostles' work. We must shepherd the multitudes which are distressed and scattered, and bring the life and love of God by our own Spirit-filled personality into the mind and heart of the individual. It is only by pastoral work that the world can be saved.

A minister can scamp his pastoral work and still retain his position as the shepherd of the flock, but he cannot retain his position in God's Kingdom. . Men shirk pastoral service not because they are strong, but because they are weak. They have not sufficient strength to bend their life to the life of Christ. When a man says, I hate pastoral work, and do as little of it as I can—if he had ears to hear, he could hear the Spirit saying: "Thou fool!"

(The Minister As Shepherd)

In that same volume, Dr. Jefferson analyzes the Christian Pastor's work by comparing it to the work of the Eastern Shepherd. The Christian Shepherd is a watchman; a guard; a guide; a physician to the sheep; a savior who leads in rescue work; a feeder of the sheep; and a lover of the sheep.

Quite naturally, therefore, at the heart of the work of the pastor is the idea of vicarious suffering. Because the pastor loves his people, his ministry is replete with illustrations of his suffering on their behalf. Dramatically this truth is illustrated by the words which the novelist Gladys Schmitt puts into the mouth of her hero, David:

Long ago, in the hills above Bethlehem, I made a mighty name for myself because I killed a young lion that came to harry my father's sheep. It was not for the sake of the lambs and ewes that I killed the lion—it was for the glory that the slaying of a lion would bring upon my own head. But now, being utterly weary of the world and of myself, having had all things and yearning after nothing more, I still cannot lie down to sleep while the flock is left to be ravaged in the open field. I will go back to Jerusalem for the sake of the children of Jerusalem, who wept to see me depart. Before I take unto myself my everlasting rest, I will kill one lion for the sake of the sheep.   (Quoted in **David the King**)

The basic importance of the work of the pastor, the shepherd of souls, has become a growing conviction during the years of my maturing ministry. May I speak utterly personally at this point? Perhaps it will help some of you who stand at the threshold of your Christian ministries. As I left theological seminary

one of my consuming desires seemed to be to become
a popular minister—the kind of a minister that *everybody* likes and nearly everybody comes to hear preach.
Then after a few years on the "ecclesiastical merry-go-
round" I got the ambition to be the minister of a great
church. I began to think it would be wonderful if my
name could be linked not merely with a First Church
but with a "Very First Church." Passing through that
stage I found myself, for a brief time, thinking in
terms of administrative leadership in some phase of
denominational work. But I can honestly confess that
now I have but one consuming passion as a Christian
minister—I want to be the spiritual leader of the people
that I am called upon to serve, I want to be spiritually
helpful to all those who need me. I can truthfully say
that it is in those hours when I try to help people
spiritually that I feel most like "a good minister of
Jesus Christ."

I share the sentiments of Ralph Centiman in these
lines—

"I do not ask that crowds may throng the temple,
That standing room be at a price;
I only ask that as I voice the message,
They may see Christ.

I do not ask that men may sound my praises,
Or headlines spread my name abroad;
I only pray that as I voice the message,
Hearts may find God.

I do not ask for earthly place or laurel,
Or of this world's distinction any part;
I only pray that I may show to others
My Saviour's heart."

The Apostle Paul had the heart and ministry of a
Pastor. The first Chapter of his epistle to the Colossians reveals "a Pastor's Prayer for His People." I de-
light in studying that chapter in the paraphrased words
of J. B. Phillips. The heart of that pastoral prayer is
simply this: "We are constantly praying for you."
And what is the content of that pastoral prayer?
Listen to the spiritual heart-throbs of that great pastor
for his people:

- "That you may see things from Christ's point of
view"

  "That in your outward lives men may see Christ"
- "That you will be strengthened from God's bound-
less resources"

  "That you will find yourselves able to pass
through any experience"

  "That you maintain a firm position in the faith—
do not allow yourselves to be shifted away"

  "That you may be brought to your full maturity
in Christ"
- "That you may be encouraged"
- "That you may find out more and more how
strong are the bonds of Christian love"

  "That you may grow more certain in your knowledge of God"

  "That you may grow more sure in your grasp of
God"

  "That your spiritual experience may grow richer"

And so today the Christian Minister finds himself to be "The Modern Shepherd."

"The Master told of a shepherd true
Who counted his sheep at the close of the day
And found one lost—so the whole night through
He sought till he found the one astray.
From out of the night and the storm he came
To the safe corral, with a joy elate,
And calling the lost by its chosen name
He placed it inside the wicket gate.

'Tis a simple story He told them then,
And a simple task that the shepherd had.
The Master, a Shepherd Himself to men,
Gave proof of His love for his lost and sad.
But shepherds He sets o'er His flocks today
Find their work complex and the journey long.
The lost are many and dawn is grey
Ere their work is done with the human throng.

The shepherd who sought for that one lost sheep
Thought not of himself till the lost was found—
Oh Shepherd of shepherds Thy vigil keep
In us Thy shepherds the whole year round;
That everywhere in the world of men
In the stress of these complex modern days
We may make the parable live again,
Hear the Shepherd's voice, learn the Shepherd's
    ways."

(Charles N. Pace)

There are many areas of true spiritual leadership on the part of the pastor. To begin with, the minister becomes the spiritual leader of his people by the very quality of his own life and by the spiritual ideal for his church toward which he strives constantly. Nothing is more important than the minister's own personal spiritual example. For if the preacher is a teacher of teachers and a leader of leaders, he is also an example of examples. Dr. Gerald McCullough suggests that if a minister is to stand up *under* his people and stand up *to* his people, and stand up *for* his people, he must, first of all, stand up *among* his people. The high quality of the minister's own spiritual life is a requisite for his effective spiritual leadership.

Such personal spiritual example on the part of ministers is the New Testament ideal. The Apostle Paul recognized this over and over again in his pastoral ministry. To the Thessalonian Christians he wrote: "As ye know what manner of men we were among you, for your sake; and ye became followers of us and of the Lord." (I Thessalonians 1:5, 6.) "Ye are witnesses and God also—how holily and justly and unblameably we behaved ourselves among you." (I Thessalonians 2:10.) To young Timothy Paul was able to write: "Howbeit for this cause I obtained mercy, that in me first Jesus Christ might show forth all longsuffering, for a pattern to them which should hereafter believe on Him to life everlasting." (I Timothy 1:16.)

Little wonder is it then that St. Paul exhorted Timothy and Titus, as ministers, in such words as these: "Let no man despise thy youth; but be thou an example of the believers, in word, in conversation, in charity, in spirit, in faith, in purity." (I Timothy 4:12.) "In all things showing thyself a pattern of good works." (Titus 2:7.)

The spiritual leadership on the part of the minister is, likewise, constantly being felt as his people come under the influence of his lofty spiritual goals for the church. The minister whose pastoral ideal is to "let the church be the church" and who constantly leads in that spiritual direction, is truly a spiritual leader of his people. There is an interesting story told about the late Bishop Quayle who one day was traveling in his typical non-clerical attire on a railroad train. His only companion, who was a salesman, and who began to believe that the Bishop was also a salesman, said to him during the course of the conversation: "And what, may I ask, do you sell, sir?" To which, with a whimsical smile on his face, the Bishop answered: "I am selling horizons."

How very true it is—as the minister demonstrates personally a high quality of spiritual life, and as he sets lofty spiritual goals for his church, he is "selling spiritual horizons"—and after all, this is the most effective kind of spiritual leadership.

In the second place, the minister is the spiritual leader of his people in his conduct of corporate worship. I am thinking primarily of two things: the actual conduct and content of the public worship services; and the preaching which is done at those services. I am not intending to enter into a detailed discussion of

Christian public worship. Theoretically, I am not a specialist in liturgics and worship-techniques. But, speaking in an extremely practical vein, I think that I understand the spiritual significance of public worship and know much about the minister's responsibility to make such public worship spiritually significant.

Unfortunately I must confess that much corporate worship in Protestant circles is conducted ineffectively, for the most part. Too often worship services either are not prepared for at all, or are illy-prepared for, by the minister; and the result is a churchly sloppiness, an intellectual boredom, and a spiritual vacuum. I am one who believes that we should truly follow the scriptural exhortation and worship the Lord in the *beauty* of holiness.

I follow a few basic principles in trying to fulfil my pastoral responsibility for leading public worship. First, I believe that every public worship service is a spiritual opportunity. That particular service may be the occasion of God's visitation upon an individual or individuals within the congregation or upon the congregation as a whole. Therefore, let me say, with apologies to the marriage ritual, no public worship service is ever to "be entered into unadvisedly, but reverently, discreetly, and in the fear of God."

Secondly, I think that the public worship service should be planned as a unit, or unity. Every worship service should have a specific spiritual purpose, and each item in the service should make a definite contribution to the total purpose. Hymns, anthems, scripture readings, etc., should be aimed at helping to accomplish the desired spiritual objective.

In the third place, I believe that each portion of the minister's conduct of the worship service should be done well. The scriptures should be read well; the prayers should be given well; the announcements should be made well; and the sermon should be preached well—all for the glory of God! If God expects our best in time and talent and treasure, He also expects the minister's best in the conduct of public worship.

Public worship should be conducted so well, under the influence of God's spirit, that worshippers will have real communion with God during it, and as a result of it will sense a new revelation of God's truth and grace for their daily lives. How spiritually tragic are those so-called worship services which fail to influence the attendants spiritually. One day, during that period when Mahatma Gandhi was trying to make up his mind religiously, he attended a Wesleyan Church service. But he was totally unimpressed by it. Concerning such a spiritual tragedy one has written: "A Wesleyan Church drowsy and dull at a moment when one of the world's greatest men sat in the pews and was slowly making up his mind."

Undoubtedly, the most important planned-for item in public worship is the sermon. I follow the early Protestant tradition which holds that the minister in public worship is basically a prophet, rather than a priest (and such a statement does not minimize my appreciation of the priestly functions of a minister). I hold in the highest regard the value of the pulpit in the minister's spiritual leadership of his people. What the minister thinks and speaks becomes an important part of his spiritual leadership. Preaching is ministerial leadership by means of the declaration of spiritual principles and the utterance of theological, social and ethical convictions.

In a recent "Sermon or Sanctuary" contest, sponsored by the former Methodist "Christian Advocate," contestants were asked to write whether the sermon or the parts of the worship service other than the sermon influenced their spiritual lives more. There were sent in 1,364 essays, representing every state in the U. S. A., the District of Columbia, Hawaii, Alaska, and England. One thousand people voted for the sermon as the greater spiritual influence, 350 voted for the sanctuary and fourteen voted for both.

But admitting all of this which makes the sermon by a Christian Minister so signally significant, the contemporary preacher finds himself in somewhat of a "plight." For one thing, church programs which are supposed to be carried out, usually to the very letter of the law, are giving him less and less time both for the preparation and for the delivery of sermons.

Moreover, the contemporary prophet-preacher finds his hearers in a strange new world quite different from that in which the seeds of prophetic preaching burst forth in the days of the Reformation. The prophet's role in Luther's day was primarily to individuals-in-their-relationship-to-God and this considered almost apart from social relationships. In our day the prophet's concern is with individuals who are so much a complex part of a highly-secularized society that to try to extricate them is both meaningless and impossible.

Let the minister remember that in his preaching he is the spiritual leader of his people. He must speak for God to people who need God, who seemingly need Him more because of the complexities of contemporary life. Relying totally upon the revelations of Holy Scripture the minister must declare "timeless truth for timely hours."

There is a third basic consideration in this matter of a minister's spiritual leadership of his people: the minister is the spiritual leader of his people as he through pastoral counseling mediates the Grace of God to personal needs. When I refer to Pastoral Counseling I am thinking of any situation, either in the home or office of the person seeking help, or in the office or counseling room of the minister, when an individual confronts the minister with a specific personal solution to it.

I am convinced that this matter of spiritual counseling by the minister is an essential in any effective Christian ministry today. The primary purpose of the minister is not the promotion of programs but the production of spiritual personalities.

It seems to me that any Christian minister who wishes to be spiritually successful in pastoral counseling must be guided by at least three spiritual principles. He must believe, first of all, that the will of God for each human personality is whole-ness. I am impressed by the title of a recent theological volume "Holiness is Whole-ness." Moreover, the spiritual counselor must understand clearly that in the realm of human personality, just as in every other area of God's creation, there is constantly operative the law of cause and effect. There is always a reason for personality-maladies, whether they be in the realm of the mind, the emotions, or the will. A third principle makes the difficult work of the spiritual counselor glorious: it is the conviction that the Grace of God is adequate for every human need.

The minister must be the kind of a man, in personality and spirituality, that people will want to counsel with him and will approach him without hesitation and with confidence. It is tragically unfortunate when ministers give the impression of an unrelenting stiffness of bearing, of a heartless indifference to human needs, and of having attained a superior realm of existence to that experienced by so-called "ordinary" people. Needy people will not bring their personal problems to "stuffed shirts."

The minister who will be asked to give spiritual counsel is the one who has already shown his willingness to help by his attitude of real interest in people, and his loving concern for their problems and needs. To some, other people are merely objects. To yet others, people are viewed as objects emotionally needful to them. But to those who give spiritual counsel and guidance people are persons in whom there is genuine interest and for whom there is sincere Christian concern. It was such an interest in people that impelled John Wesley to learn to know his people personally:

"On the following days I spoke with each member of the society in Kingswood. I cannot understand how any minister can hope ever to give up his account with joy, unless (as Ignatius advises) he knows all his flock by name; not overlooking the men-servants and maid-servants." (*Journal*)

The spiritual counselor will manifest the spirit of sympathy and patience in his dealings with people. "The servant of the Lord must not strive; but be gentle unto all men, apt to teach, patient, in meekness instructing those that oppose themselves." (II Timothy 2:24, 25.) How patient the counselor must be: "or ministry, let us wait on our ministering." (Romans 12:7.)

What a demonstration of effective pastoral oversight and care the Apostle Paul gave to his spiritual children in the various churches. "Watching like a proud father the solid steadfastness of your faith in Christ." (Colossians 2:5—Phillips.) "But we were gentle among you, even as a nurse cherisheth her children." (I Thessalonians 2:7, 8.) "As ye know how we exhorted and comforted and charged every one of you, as a father doth his children." (I Thessalonians 2:19, 20.) "For now *we* love if *ye* stand fast in the Lord." (I Thessalonians 3:8.)

The minister, as spiritual counselor, must be able to diagnose and interpret human problems and perplexities. The minister must be a specialist in personal and human relations. May I give in very general terms three illustrations from my own ministry in which the ability to diagnose and interpret made it possible to help people spiritually.

A young lady who had made a profession of faith in Christ was taking instruction for church membership. One of the assignments I gave to her was to read the Gospel according to St. Mark in its entirety. When I met with her the next time I questioned her concerning her reading and asked what impressed her most in her reading. Her immediate reply was that she could not get over the fact that Jesus Christ was so forgiving. She remarked, "Why Jesus Christ forgave everybody for everything." Within a very few minutes I was able to discover that this young lady was harboring a spirit of non-forgiveness in her heart. Many years before her brother had wronged her and she was determined never to forgive him. And so, I as her minister was given the opportunity not only to teach her the secret of forgiveness but to help her apply it.

A young man who was a moral and spiritual victim of World War II came to me suffering with mental depression and inferiority because of some men with whom he worked, yet none of the men had wronged or slighted him in any way. It's a long story, and it was a tedious counseling process. But wise counseling and sympathetic understanding finally laid hold of the real cause of the man's problem—deep personal guilt because of moral irregularities during all the war years. You see, the trouble he experienced at work was only a neurological manifestation of an inner spiritual malady. The wise counselor must learn how to deal with root-causes, not mere symptoms. When this man's guilt was cleansed by Jesus Christ his whole life was changed and he has become fully adjusted in all the relationships of his life.

I think so often of the young mother who came to talk with me about joining the church. But we got nowhere in our discussions. Finally, realizing that her problem was far deeper than a normal desire to join a church, I began probing into the depths of her soul. And there it was—moral guilt festering in the soul for ten years, even though during all of that time her nearest friends told her she had nothing to worry about. Church membership took care of itself when she became a new creature in Jesus Christ.

If the minister wants to help people he will have to understand people, and the best school for understanding people is pastoral experience. Truly the best way to become an effective spiritual counselor is to counsel, and to keep on counseling.

But having diagnosed and interpreted personal problems and human needs, the minister must be skilled in his ability to prescribe the Grace of Jesus Christ so that it will be intimately and effectively applicable to human needs. Here the skill of the "physicians of souls" is demanded. A minister doesn't just mouth words when he is confronted by one who is face to face with the elemental facts and the grim realities of life. This is the time to offer a spiritual remedy that actually works. We have often sung:

"Here bring your wounded hearts,
here tell your anguish;
Earth has no sorrow that
Heaven cannot heal."

(Thomas Moore)

But the spiritual counselor has to prescribe for an individual the spiritual treatment by which the sorrows of Earth are actually healed by Heaven. In every spiritual case, just as in the realm of the physical, diagnosis must be followed by therapeutics. And on the basis of one's response to the suggested therapeutics the counselor is able to make a usually satisfactory prognosis.

The minister as spiritual counselor must show people how to get the best of guilt, of temptation, of self-centeredness, of fear, of doubt, of despair, of anger, of criticism, of suffering, of ill-will, of sin, of disappointment, of inferiority, of jealousy, of pride, of tensions, of failure, of discontent, and of any other malady of the human personality which prevents an individual from living triumphantly.

And having helped people gain the initial victory over these enemies of the soul and of the personality, the spiritual counselor must lead these same people from spiritual victory to spiritual victory until the new pattern of mastery in and through Christ becomes the established pattern of one's life.

The significance of such a ministry in which pastoral counseling plays so prominent a part is discovered in the fact that such a ministry constantly speaks to life *out of* life itself. The minister's *concern* for souls leads him into a constant *care* for souls which is characterized by the continual offering of the *cure* for souls. Such a ministry is vital—life-speaking, life-appealing, life-healing—and hence it is valid.

The Rev. A. Powell Davies, in his review of the book, *"A Man Called Peter,"* says of the hero—

Of Peter Marshall more than of most, it may be said that his thought came out of his life. He was sometimes sensitive . . to what he felt to be the limitations of his scholarship. This should never have troubled him. His special talent was for seeing life through the insights prompted by his own experience. Since his experience was rich and varied and always intense from the ardor of his own fervent temperament, he could draw upon it almost inexhaustibly and it became the link between the eternal verities of his Christian convictions and the problems of the people to whom he spoke.

When the minister is at heart a spiritual counselor and guide, even his preaching will be life-conditioned. Such a preacher will speak to life just where he finds it and seek to lead it just where Jesus Christ wants it. The following words concerning "What A Preacher Sees From His Pulpit Each Sunday" express the very heart-throb and passion of the preacher who is a true pastor as he faces his congregation Sunday after Sunday:

There are Lost Souls before us—souls going down to eternal death without Christ, and we are trying to rescue them.

There are Young People before us who, in Folly's Court and the Carnal Pleasure's Mart are flinging away the wealth God gave them at the start, and we are trying to get them to see the error of such a way.

There are Old People before us—old people facing the sunset of life, who are not yet ready to meet God, and we try to get them ready to answer the inevitable summons.

There are Some before us who may be suddenly snatched out of the world by accident or disease, even as some are every day, and we try to bring them to the way of faith and life that would make them ready to face eternity if, in a moment, in the twinkling of an eye, they were taken from us.

There are Those before us who live the life of sinful pleasure—dancing to the music of self-indulgence, chasing the short-lived butterflies of pleasure, and we try to get them to live more for the other world than for the transient things of this world.

There are Wanderers before us—prodigals who have gone into the far country, and are at the Devil's hog trough, wasting the precious things of life in riotous living, and we try to bring them back to penitence and to the Father's house.

There is Some Man who is living in impurity, or making his marriage vows perpetual perjury, and we try to bring him out of his bondage and night into Christ's freedom and light.

There are a Number who live prayerless lives, lives without faith, lives that lack zeal, and we try to bring them to the prayer closet, to believe in God, to service in God's cause.

Somebody's Boy has wandered, and we want to bring him back to honor, home, and parents and God.

Somebody's Girl has lost hold of herself and the best ideals, and we try to anchor her lest she drift into the shallows of life.

There is Somebody who is sad, Somebody discouraged, Somebody unappreciated, and we don't want to give them a stone when they need bread. (R. G. Lee, quoted in **Western Christian Advocate**)

Perhaps it would be fitting to close this discussion on pastoral counseling by quoting what Mark M. Moore calls "The Ten Commandments of Pastoral Counseling":

"(1) Thou shalt seek to understand.
(2) Thou shalt put thyself in the other person's place.
(3) Thou shalt love people and be sympathetic.
(4) Thou shalt not be easily shocked.
(5) Thou shalt be a good listener.
(6) Thou shalt not talk too much.
(7) Thou shalt not over-simplify the problem.
(8) Thou shalt not minimize sin and evil.
(9) Thou shalt never betray a confidence.
(10) Thou shalt attempt seriously to bring God into the experience."

Thus far, we have discussed three ways in which the minister is the spiritual leader of his people: in the quality of his own spiritual life and the spiritual goals he sets for his church; in his conduct of corporate worship and his preaching; and in his work of pastoral counseling.

The minister is, likewise, the spiritual leader of his people in the work of Evangelism. While it is true that most church leaders will admit, at least theoretically, that evangelism is the chief business of the church, it is just as true that the basic meaning of evangelism must be re-studied and re-discovered in our modern church. In recent years I have viewed with alarm what I consider to be an emerging new concept of evangelism in the Protestant Church. Too many are prone to believe that evangelism is synonymous with just about everything the Church does. To those who hold this new concept Christian education and Christian social service and Christian worship are synonymous with evangelism.

But this is not the New Testament concept of evangelism. True evangelism means the confrontation of sinful men, judged guilty by the moral decrees of God, with the offer of a redeeming power, made available only through Jesus Christ, and the exhortation to such sinful men to accept at once this Redeeming Grace. Evangelism is bringing Christ to men and men to Christ. "Evangelism," as Dr. W. E. Sangster defines it, "is going to the people outside. It is the proclamation of the good news of God in Jesus Christ to 'them that are without.' It is the sheer work of the herald who goes in the name of the King to the people who, either openly or by their indifference, deny their allegiance to their rightful Lord." (*Let Me Commend,* p. 14.)

Do not misunderstand me: Christian worship should be evangelistic, but in itself it is not evangelism. Christian education should be evangelistic, but in itself it is not evangelism. Christian social service should be evangelistic, but in itself it is not evangelism. Christian Evangelism is a specific area of Christian activity and it has its own well-defined objectives.

The Christian minister must "do the work of an evangelist." (II Timothy 4:5.) And in the same verse Paul reminds Timothy that he will "make full proof of his ministry" only as he does the work of an evangelist. The minister must be an evangelist himself. The spirit of his life and ministry must be evangelistic. The goals which he sets for his church must be built upon a firm foundation of evangelism. The minister must engage in personal evangelism in his parish. Remember the words of Christ to Paul at the time of his conversion and Divine Call—"I have appeared unto thee for this purpose, to make thee . . . a witness both of these things which thou hast seen, and of those things in the which I will appear unto thee." (Acts 26:16.)

The minister must lead his people in all forms of evangelism: personal evangelism; public evangelism; visitation evangelism; and all other forms deemed practical for particular situations. Think how valuable a series of training sessions, conducted by the minister, on the topic, "How to Be a Personal Evangelist," would be to every local church. I, likewise, believe sincerely in regular series of revival meetings, or evangelistic services. As pastor I feel that my responsibility toward such special series of services is at least two-fold: first, I must insist that the right kind of evangelist is brought into my church. And, secondly, I must do everything possible to prepare my church spiritually for the coming of the evangelist and for the special meetings.

Furthermore, it is my opinion that the minister has the responsibility at times of being his own evangelist. The preacher should preach many definitely evangelistic sermons in the course of a year's regular ministry. And occasionally he should conduct his own series of evangelistic services and do the preaching.

What is evangelistic preaching? It is like other types of preaching in that it is truth expressed through personality and is the proclamation of the Gospel of

Jesus Christ. But it is unlike other types of preaching in that it is truth directed at the non-Christian or un-Christian and it strives for an immediate decision for Christian discipleship. An evangelistic sermon is one that brings the hearer face-to-face with Jesus Christ as the Son of God and moves upon him to accept Jesus Christ now as Saviour and Lord.

There are at least five characteristics of evangelistic preaching. It is Biblical in substance. It is usually doctrinal in content. It deals with the great Christian doctrines of sin, salvation, and judgment. It is personal, for evangelistic preaching should make each man feel as though he is the only one for whom Christ died. Such preaching should do three things for the individual. It gives him the *intellectual* element in faith; and thus it persuades him to *believe* in the Lord Jesus Christ as his Saviour. It gives him the *emotional* element in faith; and thus it persuades him to *want* to accept Christ as Saviour. It gives him the *volitional* element in faith; and thus it persuades him to *accept* Christ as Saviour.

Evangelistic preaching is impassioned. An infidel lawyer said to a young preacher who had come to interview him, "If I believed what you claim to believe, I could not take it as lightly as you do. I would not rest day nor night. I would warn men and plead with them to be saved. If I pleaded my cases like you present Christ, I would lose all of them."

Because of all of this, evangelistic preaching is difficult and demanding, and only the preacher who gives his best to the assignment and who relies utterly and constantly upon the Holy Spirit can hope to succeed.

One of the most widely-used forms of evangelism in the modern church is that known as Visitation Evangelism. It is the method by which trained personal evangelists go in teams of two into the homes of those who are outside of Christ and the Church and seek to win them to a personal faith in Christ and to an active relationship to the Church. I have used this method of Visitation Evangelism often, and with great spiritual profit to my churches. The secret of Visitation Evangelism is to make sure that in its content as well as its method it is patterned after New Testament evangelism.

As I see it there are five definite stages in the program of Visitation Evangelism, which I shall merely mention and not discuss in detail. First, there must be compiled an active PROSPECT LIST. A list of all those who should be won to Christ and His Church, for whom a local Church is responsible, must be kept up-to-date at all times. Second, there must be the SELECTION OF VISITORS. The lay people who are to do the work of evangelism in the homes of the community must be "hand-picked," and this should usually be done by the minister himself.

Third, the selected workers must be carefully TRAINED by the minister. In this matter of visitation evangelism I am afraid that we take too much for granted. It is my experience that the visitors, as dedicated as they are, need thorough training for the task, and that training sessions should be held at regular intervals during any continuing program of visitation evangelism.

Fourth, the actual VISITING must be done, and this I believe to be accomplished more effectively when it follows a definite schedule in the program of the church. Perhaps a church will decide to conduct Visitation Evangelism a certain night each week, or one night every month, or during an entire week three or four times a year. Definite decisions for Christ and the Church are to be sought during the visits.

The final stage is that of the FOLLOW-UP WORK. This has three stages: (1) The minister must confirm all decisions for Christ and conduct whatever instruction for Church membership is deemed necessary. (2) The minister must conduct a meaningful ceremony of reception into the Church. (3) The most important task of all is the assimilation of the new members into the fellowship and worship and activities of the Church.

It is imperative that the minister be the spiritual leader of his people in Evangelism. This is true not only from the nature of the work of the Christian Ministry itself but also because the contemporary church faces an unprecedented opportunity for evangelism. Look at the evangelistic challenge in our nation alone. There will be a net gain of more than 63 million people in this country during the next twenty years. And add to this the fact there are now more unchurched people in the U.S.A.—nearly 70 millions of them—than was our total population in 1890. The Christian Church must evangelize or die!

I want to mention briefly one other area in which the minister must be the spiritual leader of his people. The minister must lead his people into a more adequate understanding of, a greater interest in, and a more dedicated support of Christian Missions. In spite of the fact that the Early Church was born in a missionary crusade and that the greatest periods of expansion and progress in the history of the Christian Church have been during those times of intense missionary activity, yet it remains a difficult task to interest vitally the average church member today in the program of world evangelization. That this is true is evident from the low per capita of giving to missions in the major Protestant denominations. Too many church members are like the prominent businessman who in handing me a check for the church, commented, "Preacher, use this money any way you want except for missions."

How can the local minister be the leader of his people in Christian Missions? I would suggest that, first of all, he must be "thoroughly sold" on Christian Missions himself. It doesn't take very long for church people to discover just what things their minister is vitally interested in. It takes a missionary spirit in the pulpit to keep alive missionary interest in the pew.

The minister must also make Christian Missions a recurring topic in his preaching. The Bible is a great missionary book. Some of the grandest passages in the Holy Scriptures are thrilling missionary texts. And then, of course, Christian history and Christian biography are replete with inspiring illustrations of the tremendous influence of Christian Missions around the world.

I would make a third suggestion concerning the development of a truly Christian interest in missions on the part of the local church. I believe that annually each local church should conduct either a School of Missions or a Missionary Conference. Such an event in the life of the church enables the people of the church to be influenced by a concentrated emphasis upon missions during a particular period of time.

In my church we have an annual Missionary Conference. A recent Missionary Conference included two entire Sundays and four week-nights in between. Regular services with guest missionaries were held, with the exception of Saturday night when a Church Family Covered Dish Supper was held with guest missionaries in attendance who shared with us informally concerning their missionary activities. I am convinced that such a missionary conference—with eight missionary services being held within eight days and with missionaries from around the world in attendance—makes an invaluable contribution to the cause of Christian Missions in the local Church.

A School of Missions in the local church is usually held on consecutive weeks, instead of on consecutive days. A day or a night each week for a month is devoted to the holding of classes in Christian Missions for the various age groups. These classes are taught by missionaries, or by missionary leaders in the local churches. Sometimes the regular mission study books are used. Each session of a School of Missions usually has a public assembly for all those attending, at which time a missionary speaks.

It seems to me that one of the best ways to increase missionary interest and activity in the local church is to personalize Christian Missions just as much as possible. People are interested only in what and whom they actually know. Church people need to know missionaries and to know just what they are doing for Christ and His Church. And many times people will give much, much more, to specific missionary projects that they personally know about.

The Christian Church of tomorrow will only be as strong as is its missionary spirit today. Our age presents an unparalleled opportunity for world evangelization. And this unparalleled opportunity is crucial—both for the Church and for the world. For at the moment we are compelled to admit this sobering fact —that the contemporary church, in its self-complacency and spiritual indifference, has permitted the initiative in the battle for the minds and souls of men to pass into non-Christian hands. Will the Christian Church seize the initiative in world evangelization soon again? Undoubtedly the answer is to be found in the local minister and in the local church, for a denomination can be no more effective in world evangelization than its local churches permit it to be.

Thus, we have considered some of the outstanding areas in which the minister must be the spiritual leader of his people: by the quality of his own spiritual life and by the spiritual goals he holds for his church; in his leadership of public worship and in his preaching; in the work of evangelism and of missions; and in the whole area of pastoral counseling.

The minister dare not fail in this matter of spiritual leadership. In his dedication to the work of the Christian ministry, in his reliance upon the Grace of God whose power is realized through mighty intercession, and in his undying love for all those for whom Christ died, he must be "a workman who is not ashamed" in his spiritual leadership of his people. For after all, this is the crucial area in a man's ministry. His prime concern must always be with the souls of men. He is called primarily to help develop maturing spiritual life within those to whom he ministers; and if he fails in this matter, any other areas of so-called ministerial success will not ultimately matter.

In order that we may be seriously challenged anew to be spiritual leaders of the people we are called upon to serve, permit me to share with you a confession which a minister shared with his fellow-ministers:

Not in more than thirty years as a minister of the Gospel have I felt so complete a sense of failure. The hours have grown into days and soon the days will grow into a week, and nothing that I have been able to do has taken away the feeling of frustration that has settled down on me. Of course, it cannot last with this intensity, but while it lasts I am hoping that I will learn something that will keep me from failing next time.

As I walked down the street, a man said, "They have just brought in a body over there. It is a young lady. I knew you would want to know." I walked over to the funeral parlors. The lady attendant said, "The body is still in the hearse. If you wish, you may look and see if she is one of your members." Gently, I laid the sheet back and looked into the face of an eighteen-year-old girl. Death had not erased the beauty. A majesty of calmness had replaced the radiant smile that always shone on her face. And I knew as I looked that tragedy was written over that untimely end of life. How I felt a sense of sinking in my soul!

Somehow I felt that she understood me, when I whispered, "Listen, child, somewhere I have failed you. If I had been the minister that I should, that radiant smile that I saw on your face this morning would not have changed to this! You would have come to me to tell me about your dilemma, if I had been the minister that I should have been."

Instead she had sought desperate means and had died. Perhaps within a flash as fast as that of lightning her spirit had gone. Not a suicide, no. She had sought the aid of one who was a renegade to his calling. There were police proceedings and brutal publicity.

To the soft tones of religious music, and to the stately tones of the ritual, we gave to her all that we could give—after we had failed so miserably in life, we gave her the best we could in death.

"I never saw her when she was not smiling." This was an expression that came frequently when she died. Somehow, that smiling face has been haunting me like a ghost.

Somehow, I have felt that I wanted to scream out to my people and say, "Where have I failed? Why did she not come to the preacher and seek his guidance? Shepherd? Minister? Pastor? How can one use these terms who has failed to make people feel that he can lead them to One who can bring an answer even to life's worst dilemmas?

Today, all alone, I walked back to the little cemetery lot. The flowers had faded. Without embarrassment I confess, I made no effort to restrain the tears. I let them flow. I had heard a rather thoughtless word said during the morning hour—a criticism by one who never fought life's hard fights. It sickened me, and I walked to the grave side.

Again, as I stood there, I said, "Listen, child, it's too late maybe—or maybe it isn't. Anyhow, I am sorry. I have been a failure. If I had been the minister I should have been and if my church had been the church it should have been—I wonder if this would have happened?

Through the tears that made my eyes a bit misty, I saw her face again. It was not the quiet face of death. She smiled as she did on the morning when I saw her last in life. Somehow I felt that perhaps she understood me better now, and that she forgave. I felt better. But I prayed and said, "Lord, let me not fail again one of Thy little ones. Make me such a minister that they will turn to me because they will feel that I can lead them to You." (Rev. J. O. J. Taylor)

And let me add this further prayer: "And please, Lord, help me be the kind of a minister who will never be ashamed in his spiritual leadership of his people."

CHAPTER VI

NOT ASHAMED—IN HIS MINISTRY OF HEALING

"The Spirit of the Lord is upon Me, because He hath anointed Me to preach the gospel to the poor; He hath sent Me to heal the broken hearted, to preach deliverance to the captives, and recovering of sight to the blind, to set at liberty them that are bruised, to preach the acceptable year of the Lord."
(Luke 4:18, 19)

Everywhere in the religious world there is a resurgence of interest in the relationship between religion and health, between faith and healing. This is evident, first of all, in the realm of medical science, for today physicians and psychiatrists alike are stressing the importance of psycho-somatic medicine in their treatment of patients.

This is likewise true in the religious world. During the past quarter of a century several of the major Protestant denominations throughout the world have established special commissions on spiritual healing, and there are in some instances particular healing movements within the framework of the denomination. It is interesting to note that a recent survey conducted by the National Council of Churches reveals that 34 per cent of Protestant ministers attempt spiritual healing. And, of course, this revival of concern about healing on the part of Protestants has focused fresh attention on certain of the great healing centers, such as Lourdes, operated by the Roman Catholics. Moreover, books on religion and healing are coming in increasing numbers from the pens of religious scholars and teachers of varied religious persuasions.

Then outside the framework of the major denominations there are being carried on today many healing movements of far reaching proportions. I suppose that the most widely-known of these is that being carried on by the Rev. Oral Roberts, Pentecostal preacher and faith healer, whose purchased time on radio and TV now blankets 667 stations per week. I quote from an editorial comment about Oral Roberts and his faith healing:

One comes away from this half-hour TV spectacular vaguely disturbed and fascinated. The man is utilizing a genuine and recognized power. The connection between prayer and health is widely conceded, and a resurgence of interest in this phenomenon is spreading throughout the churches today. Some persons apparently are gifted in healing and Oral Roberts quite possibly possesses this gift.

But how he uses it! No gentle laying on of hands is to be seen in his techniques. Roberts slaps his patients on the brow or the face; and his far-from-reverent prayers shout at God with imperatives: "Lord, when I put this child down, he's got to walk." Then the child gets off the healer's lap and runs away on once-useless legs. (Quoted in **The Presbyterian**)

In view of all this contemporary resurgence of interest in the matter of religion and healing it appears to me that a two-fold responsibility devolves upon the minister at this point: first, he must seek to discover and understand what is the true relationship between religion and health, between faith and healing; and, second, he must include in his total ministry to people a sane and scriptural ministry of spiritual healing. It would seem to me that if a minister is to be "a workman that needeth not to be ashamed" he must not be ashamed in his ministry of healing.

What do we mean by healing? As far as I am concerned, Dr. Leslie D. Weatherhead has given the most adequate definition in these words:

Healing is the process of restoring the broken harmony which prevents personality, at any point of body, mind, or spirit, from its perfect functioning in its relevant environment; the body in the material world; the mind in the realm of true ideas; the spirit in its relationship to God. (**Psychology, Religion and Healing, p. 464**)

To me the logic of a healing ministry is three-fold. First, there is the psychological logic of healing. The human personality is created in the image of God. There is a deep unity within the human personality— a vital relationship which manifests itself in a constant interplay and inter-reaction between mind and spirit and body. Since we hold a theistic conception of the universe we believe in a personal and continuing relationship of the Creator to the created; and truly this relationship at its loftiest level is one of life-imparting power and of life-responding receptivity. Jesus Christ is the Alpha and Omega of human personality. As E. Stanley Jones has commented: "Life will work in God's way and in no other. The blood stream, the cells, the muscles, the tissues, the biological functions —all are made to work in God's way."

The logic of a healing ministry is also theological. Here I have reference to the healing ministry of Jesus

Christ. He was truly the Great Physician—He performed far more miracles of healing than of any other kind.
"And Jesus went about all Galilee, teaching in their
synagogues, and preaching the Gospel of the Kingdom
and healing all manner of sickness and all manner of
disease among the people." (Matthew 4:23.) Jesus
said to His disciples, "As you go, preach, saying, the
Kingdom of Heaven is at hand. Heal the sick, cleanse
the lepers . . ." (Matthew 10:7, 8.) A young mother
asked me, "Is there anything in the New Testament
which says that Jesus Christ will continue to work
miracles of healing today?" Here was my answer: "Is
there anything in the New Testament which says that
He will not?"

The logic of a healing ministry is also historical.
The original commission to the apostles included the
ministry of healing. That healing played a prominent
part in the ministry of the early church is shown both
by a study of the New Testament Scriptures and by
the conclusions of those who have studied the post-
apostolic Church.   Evelyn Frost, author of the studious
volume *Christian Healing*, which is a study of the
Ante-Nicene fathers, beginning with Clement of Rome
(95 A.D.) and continuing to Lactantius (315 A.D.),
and their recorded references to Christian healing,
shows conclusively that healing was a significant part
of the early Church's ministry. It is interesting to
observe and undoubtedly it is more than a coincidence
that the spiritual ministry of healing in the early
Church began to "fade away" when ecclesiasticism in
the Church began to develop.

As we pursue our study of healing we must remember constantly that all healing is of God. The healing power belongs to God. Healing is never the work of demons. It is never the result of mere human knowledge or skill. Healing comes from God.

Kenneth Roberts, a well-known author, was once invited by an eminent surgeon to watch a complicated operation. Shortly beforehand the doctor seemed confident, but a little tense.

"All set?" asked Roberts.

"Almost," the doctor replied. He stopped, bowed his head for a moment, and then proceeded with the operation. His hands never faltered.

Afterwards Roberts said to him, "I was surprised at your praying before you went in. I thought a surgeon relied solely on his own ability."

The doctor answered, "A surgeon is only human. He can't work miracles by himself. I'm certain that science couldn't have advanced as far as it has, were it not for something stronger than mere man."

"You see," he concluded, "I feel so close to God when I'm operating that I don't know where my skill leaves off and His begins."

What, then, is the relationship between the Christian religion and healing? I believe it to be five-fold. In the first place, the Christian religion inspires healthy living and this is the best prevention of disease. Just suppose an individual from early in his life really lived the Christian way—would not healthy living result in most instances and much sickness be avoided?

Dr. James Buskirk in his volume, *Religion, Heal-*

ing and Health, reminds us that there are nine characteristics of the Christian way of life, all of which
contribute toward a person's health. The Christian
religion teaches and encourages the proper care of the
body. It enforces the virtue of honest work, which has
a definite therapeutic value. The Christian faith pro-
motes recreation and relaxation. It encourages a person to turn from himself and to rest in the Lord. The
Christian religion encourages Christian worship, which
also has a tremendous therapeutic effect. It encourages
the study of the Bible which becomes a marvelous
opportunity for the constructive power of suggestion
to operate upon the personality. The Christian religion
offers faith as the only antidote to fear; and it frees
the human personality from the devastating burden
of guilt. The Christian religion always says "Forgive,"
"Love one another." Such sound therapeutic advice
finds dramatic confirmation in Dr. Smiley Blanton's
latest volume, which is a study of his life as a psychiatrist, and which is revealingly entitled *Love or
Perish.*

Truly the Christian religion in its principles for
personal living and in its exhortations to life inspires
healthy living and this is the best prevention of disease.

In the second place, the healing power of the Christian religion is discovered in the fact that it aids healing through physical and psychological methods by the
creation of proper mental, emotional and spiritual attitudes within the individual. Just as healing through
physical methods is impeded by wrong mental, emotional, and spiritual attitudes, it is aided by right at-

titudes. This is clearly demonstrated in what is commonly known as "the will to live." Negatively considered, there are case records of what are called "psychological deaths." There are patients who lose interest in life, and, feeling that there is nothing worth living for, succumb to the first illness that comes along.

And even when death does not result, the process of physical or mental recovery is impeded drastically and prolongedly by wrong attitudes toward life. A noted doctor once told of the surprisingly slow recovery of a patient after a mild attack of influenza. Even though there was no physical cause for her continuing debility, she continued to have no appetite, a poor pulse, and to look unfit. Finally, it was discovered that the reason she was failing to recover normally was that she did not want to recover. If she recovered she knew she would have to return to a job which was causing her much unhappiness.

Positively speaking, it is this "will to live" which is often the deciding factor between death and recovery. An anesthetist once said: "Patients who go to the operating table with a confident faith in God take less anesthetic, recover from it more easily and with far less of the usual distressing after-effects."

Have you ever heard of "The Borrowed Timers" who lived on a ranch near Ellenburg, Washington? They are a splendid illustration of the healthful influences of right mental, emotional and spiritual attitudes. Back in 1936 Jess and Nancy Green were struggling to keep their ranch. Nancy had been given less than a year to live. She did the housework for

her husband and five children between her long rests
on the couch. Guyer D. Thomas was boarding there,
and he, too, had only a short time to live. Then a
Mrs. Bolding came to visit the Greens and told how
she could count time only in months, a bad stomach
case.

When she collapsed one day, Guyer Thomas had
a bright idea. He said, "Why not invite other invalids
in who have only a limited time to live? Each of us
has some good parts left. The 'ups' could look after
the 'downs' until the 'downs' felt like getting up. The
'ups' could work together for the support of all."
Fifteen hopeless cases were soon gathered there, all
helping one another as best they could. Then one
night when the children forgot to say their prayers,
Thomas gazed off into space for awhile and thought
of a way to remind them of Christ. He made a little
cross and covered it with luminous paint so it would
shine in the dark. Children seeing it on a dark wall
would remember it was time to talk to God. And the
afflicted members of the household, lying awake in
the long watches in the night, would find comfort in its
message.

Here was something, they agreed, that most of
them could help make and sell. There was but eighty
cents in cash in the pockets of the entire group. They
were dreadfully poor. But that eighty cents bought
some chemicals and blue felt, and nearby telephone
poles furnished cardboard left over from a recent
political campaign. They laughed heartily over the
fact that they got thirty-six crosses out of a county

clerk, and only twenty-four out of a sheriff! One of the Green children, a girl of eleven, sold all the crosses at fifteen cents each. A radio minister heard about the crosses and mentioned them in a sermon. Orders poured in. A banker loaned them one hundred dollars, and the movement was off to a grand start. Then a radio station brought Nancy Green to Hollywood for a nationwide broadcast, and since that time they have literally been swamped with orders as well as with applications for membership in the group.

The most striking thing about "The Borrowed Timers" was their mirth. As the "ups" sat around the table mounting crosses with one member detailed to read aloud or dial the radio, it was a rare quarter hour that did not produce a hearty laugh. Life itself was something to laugh about because of the way they were cheating death. *Not one member had died* after four years of work and service, although none of them expected to last the first year out! Talk about their disabilities was prohibited unless it was absolutely necessary. And when they were able to be up at all, there was plenty of nursing to be done, and plenty of crosses to be made. They literally forgot the hot breath of the grim reaper in their work and service and he seemed to have difficulty in catching up with them. By loving God and their neighbors as they loved themselves, by turning the stream of consciousness *away* from self in loving service, even those who faced death developed an *inner* stability of amazing strength.

Thus the Christian religion aids in healing through physical and psychological methods by the creation of positive and constructive mental, emotional and spiritual attitudes on the part of the patient. Serenity, patience, love, faith, hope, "the will to live,"—these, like medicine and surgery and psychiatry, are healing aids, and apart from them medical science is for the most part ineffective.

In order to make as complete as possible our analysis of the healing power of the Christian religion, we note, in the third place, the fact that there are records of cases in which faith and medical science have joined hands in the effecting of physical healing, each contributing a share not provided by the other.

Mrs. Elsie Salmon, "the Lady in White," the wife of a Methodist minister in South Africa, who is conducting a remarkable ministry of healing in various parts of the British Commonwealth, relates an unusual case in which this is illustrated. Rex, a boy in South Africa, was born with a cerebral hemorrhage, which caused spastic paralysis. For several years he was under the care of doctors, but showed no improvement. At the age of eight years he started having "black-outs" at the rate of seven a day, over a period of two years.

The parents of Rex heard of Mrs. Salmon's healing ministry and he was taken to her. After three visits the "black-outs" not only stopped altogether, but Rex improved so much in health that he was able to be taken to a famous brain specialist. The specialist stated that no brain operation could take place while the danger of "black-outs" remained. He advised that Mrs. Salmon be given six months to follow up the case, and then that Rex be returned to him.

There were no more "black-outs" and the boy was operated on fifteen months later. Not only was a growth removed, but an operation known as "hemispherectomy" was performed. "Hemispherectomy" involves the removal of half the brain on the assumption that "brain waves" in one hemisphere of the cerebrum may hamper the other hemisphere in its control of the body.

The following excerpts describing this operation and its effects upon Rex appeared in a South Africa newspaper:

A new treatment—involving the complete removal of half the brain—has been evolved at the Johannesburg General Hospital for certain forms of functional disorders of the brain giving rise to symptoms of epilepsy.

The lad was the seventh person in the world to undergo this operation, which gave hope to tens of thousands of people who suffered from similar cerebral disturbances.

Before the operation eighteen months ago, the boy was mentally retarded, and at the age of eleven years had advanced no further than Standard I (the mother's letter continues). Today, he has the intelligence of a youth of a far more advanced age than twelve years, and has been described by a well-known South African painter as an art student of definite promise. Yet before the operation the boy had been told he would never be able to draw. However, he is showing four of his paintings at a forthcoming exhibition. A report later says Rex had won three diplomas: the first prize for the student with the highest marks in the art class; second prize for the student between twelve and fifteen years of age; third prize in the open competition. This famous painter is amazed at the boy's work and says that in three years' time he will be able to hold an exhibition of his own paintings. He is now painting in oils.

Much of the skull was cut away during Rex's operation,

and an aperture of about four inches in diameter remained. The aperture was covered with a leather cap for protection. In eighteen months from the time of his operation he is to return to have a silver plate fitted permanently to the skull. However, in the meantime, he has been receiving divine healing, during which time the bone has been forming over the aperture and is now quite firm. The boy's parents know that by the time he is to return to the specialist, his healing will be complete and that he will never need the silver plate. (Quoted in Salmon, **He Heals Today,** pp. 50, 51)

The same article concludes with these meaningful words: "Much good work has been done when the medical fraternity has had the cooperation of a spiritual healer."

A fourth aspect of the healing power of the Christian Religion is revealed in its adequacy to heal those functional and organic illnesses which have a psychological basis. The rapid rise and development of the whole field of psycho-somatic medicine is an eloquent testimony on the part of contemporary medical science to the validity of this assertion of the power of the "Spirit" to effect healing.

Speaking of psychosomatic medicine, Albert E. Day writes:

The doctors know people who think they have only an ulcerated stomach but whose real ills are ulcerated emotions. Others are sure they are suffering from heart trouble. Perhaps there is a functional disturbance present, but the real difficulty often is not the heart that beats or misses a beat, but the "heart" that loves and hates and fears. Still others think they are worn out by overwork, when the truth is they are frayed out by unguessed inner conflicts. What people call sickness is often really only a trick of the subconscious self to get attention. (**An Autobiography of Prayer,** p. 148.)

There once appeared in *The British Medical Journal* this statement: "There is not a tissue in the human body wholly removed from the influence of the Spirit." Medical estimates, ranging from twenty-five to more than fifty percent, assert that this proportion of the people who visit doctors have functional ailments—sicknesses not produced by organic wrongs, but brought on by wrong mental, emotional, and spiritual states.

Dr. Joseph Hersey Pratt stated that "bushels of tonsils and teeth have been taken out of people who needed to be delivered from fears and self-centeredness and resentments in order to be well." Said a doctor to E. Stanley Jones: "If three-quarters of my patients found God, they would be well."

The eminent psychologist, Jung, wrote:

> Among all my patients in the second half of life—that is to say, over thirty-five—there has not been one whose problem in the last resort was not that of finding a religious outlook on life. It is safe to say that every one of them fell ill because he had lost that which living religions of every age had given to their followers, and none of them has been really healed who did not regain his religious outlook.
>
> (Quoted in Weatherhead, **Psychology, Religion, and Healing,** p. 389.)

A striking testimony to the importance of the Christian Religion as a medium of healing was given in London, England, some years ago. Dr. Martin Lloyd-Jones, a Harley Street specialist in diseases of the heart, gave up his medical work to become a Christian minister. He was a colleague of Lord Horder, Physician-in-Ordinary to King George VI. One day he suggested to Lord Horder, that they go through the files of all the cases they had dealt with in recent years, separating those cases who were suffering with organic diseases from those who were sick with functional disorders. It was found that only twenty-five percent of the patients had organic diseases and seventy-five percent were of the functional type. Dr. Lloyd-Jones asked Lord Horder what he thought medicine could do for that seventy-five percent, and the great physician replied, "Little or nothing. What they need most of all is religion." It was largely a result of this investigation that Dr. Martin Lloyd-Jones entered the Christian ministry.

We are told that for four thousand years Chinese physicians have recognized the importance of the human mind in the healing of the body. In China, it has been believed that a sick man has first to be freed from his fears.

Because of my personal interest in this aspect of the healing power of the Christian Religion, I have noted and collected in recent years, many articles from periodicals and newspapers which illustrate this striking relationship between the mind and emotions and spirit and the human body. The collection of such articles is growing at an amazing rate. In order to give something of a cross-section of what is being written in both secular and religious periodicals, let me summarize by listing some of the titles and headlines of the articles in my collection.

Here are some of the imposing titles: "Are Your

Troubles Psychosomatic?"; "Release from Nervous Tension: How Your Nerves can Make You Sick"; "Your Mind Can Keep You Well"; "Psychosomatics: If the Spirit is Ailing, the Flesh is Weak"; "Avoid that Breakdown"; "High-Pressure Living"; "Sick Because You Think So?"; "Arthritis May Result from Failure to Relax"; "Shoulder Pains Traced to Emotion"; "Psychological Blindness"; "Overt Anger is Established as Cause of Blood Pressure"; Worries and Peptic Ulcers"; "Stomach Illness Traced to Worry"; "World Conditions Affect Teeth"; "Cured by Hypnosis"; "Worry Can Cause Baldness or Gray Hair"; "Poison of Hate"; "Fear of Surgery May Set Off Mental Illness"; "Peace in Ten Seconds That May Change Your Life"; "The Will to Love"; "Your Heart May Play Tricks"; "When Your Mind Starts Hurting Your Health"; "Heart Medicine—The Healing Quality of Cheerfulness"; "Effect of Anger upon the Human Body"; "Faith Aids Health"; "How to Keep Well and Happy"; "Her Conversion Was Her Cure"; "Fertility After Adoption"; "Overweight Linked to Emotions"; "Coronary Thrombosis and High Emotional Tension"; "Common Psychosomatic Symptoms Can be Mistaken for the Common Cold"; "Blow-ups at Home Followed by Flare-ups of Arthritis"; "The Effect of Your Religion Upon Your Health"; "Much Bad Vision is Caused by Worry"; "Dogs Won't Worry—Can't be Used in Ulcer Experiments"; "What's Getting Under Your Skin?"; "Perfectionists Get Migraine Headaches."

The Christian Religion provides "the Power" to heal these functional and organic illnesses which have a psychological, rather than a structural basis. The Christian Religion offers the grace of the Lord Jesus Christ, which when received into human hearts and minds and lives, enables people to get rid of negative attitudes and emotions, and to become possessed by positive emotions. The Christian Religion releases to the human personality "the expulsive power of a new affection," which in turn acclimates the mind and soul for "new" emotions.

The Christian Religion replaces the negative experience of guilt with the positive realization of forgiveness; self-centeredness with consecration; fears and worries with faith; anger with self control; hatred and resentment with love; inferiority attitudes with security; the deprivation of love with a sense of both being wanted and being needed in God's universe.

Likewise, the Christian Religion both points a person in the direction of positive thinking and also enables him, through Divine Grace, to realize such "rightness" of thought and emotion.

How timeless are the words of John Wesley in this regard:

> The passions have a greater influence upon health than most people are aware of. All violent and sudden passions dispose to or actually throw people into acute disease. Till the passion which caused the disease is calmed, medicine is applied in vain.
>
> The love of God, as it is the sovereign remedy of all miseries, so in particular it effectually prevents all the bodily disorders the passions introduce, by keeping the passions themselves within due bounds; and by the unspeakable

calm serenity and tranquility it gives the mind, it becomes the most powerful of all the means of health and long life. (**Primitive Physic**)

So much illness is banished as soon as a person finds spiritual unity with God and His universe. E. Stanley Jones spoke realistically to a group of church men and doctors, when he declared: "A doctor must train spiritually as well as physically. Fifty percent of sick persons need prayer more than pills, aspiration more than aspirin, meditation more than medication."

The last aspect of the healing power of the Christian religion to be discussed is healing by the direct activity of God apart from the use of intermediary psychological or physical methods. Human experience bears eloquent testimony to healing by the direct touch of God after human skill has been unable to go any farther, after physical and psychological methods have exhausted themselves. Ofttimes when all else fails, God directly touches individuals and heals them. When we speak of healing by the direct activity of God apart from the use of intermediary psychological or physical methods, we refer to God intervening directly in a person's experience, apart from all recognizable human sources of remedy and cure, bringing to that individual healing that is clearly demonstrable, at the place of the mind, or soul, or body, or in a combination of any two of these areas of human personality, or of all three areas.

The evidence for such divine healing is voluminous. Space does not permit us to put together all the recorded and authenticated cases of such healing. We must be satisfied with but two illustrations—one scriptural, and the other contemporary.

The nature of such Christian healings is reflected in the New Testament miracle of Jesus' healing a long-suffering woman (Mark 5:25-34.) As Jesus passed along His way to the house of Jairus, in order to heal his daughter, great crowds thronged Him. In that multitude was a woman who had suffered twelve years from a hemorrhage. Though she had spent all her money on physicians, none had been able to cure her. As a last resort, she decided to seek the help of The Great Physician. She thought within herself: "If I may but touch His garment, I shall be healed." She touched Christ and immediately the flow of blood was stopped and she was cured. How blessed were the words of The Great Physician to her: "Daughter, be of good comfort: thy faith hath made thee whole."

The contemporary illustration is that of the miraculous healing of E. Stanley Jones. From the time I first read of it, I have been thrilled by it. Dr. Jones' own inimitable words tell the story best:

> The eight years of strain had brought on a nervous exhaustion and brain fatigue so that there were several collapses in India before I left for furlough. On board ship while speaking in a Sunday morning service, there was another collapse. I took a year's furlough in America. On my way back to India I was holding evangelistic meetings among the university students of the Philippine Islands at Manila. Several hundreds of these Roman Catholic students professed conversion. But in the midst of the strain of the meetings my old trouble came back. There were several collapses. I went on to India with a deepening cloud upon me. Here I was beginning a new term of service in this trying climate

and beginning it broken. I went straight to the hills upon arrival and took a complete rest for several months. I came down to the plains to try it out and found that I was just as badly off as ever. I went to the hills again. When I came down the second time I saw that I could go no further. I was at the end of my resources, my health was shattered. Here I was facing this call and task and yet utterly unprepared for it in every possible way.

I saw that unless I got help from somewhere I would have to give up my missionary career, go back to America and go to work on a farm to try to regain my health. It was one of my darkest hours. At that time I was in a meeting at Lucknow. While in prayer, not particularly thinking about myself, a Voice seemed to say, "Are you yourself ready for this work to which I have called you?" I replied: "No, Lord, I am done for. I have reached the end of my resources." The Voice replied, "If you will turn it over to me and not worry about it, I will take care of it." I quickly answered, "Lord, I close the bargain right here." A great peace settled into my heart and pervaded me. I knew it was done! Life— abundant Life—had taken possession of me. I was so lifted up that I scarcely touched the road as I quietly walked home that night. Every inch was holy ground. For days after that I hardly knew I had a body. I went through the days, working all day and far into the night, and came down to bedtime wondering why in the world I should ever go to bed at all, for there was not the slightest trace of tiredness of any kind. I seemed possessed by life and peace and rest—by Christ himself.

The question came as to whether I should tell this. I shrank from it, but felt I should—and did. After that it was sink or swim before everybody. But nine of the most strenuous years of my life have gone by since then, and the old trouble has never returned, and I have never had such health. But it was more than a physical touch. I seemed to have tapped new life for body, mind, and spirit. Life was on a permanently higher level. And I had done nothing but take it! **(The Christ of The Indian Road,** pp. 22-25)

What about the time since this testimony was written? Writing seventeen years later, Dr. Jones bears this further testimony to healing:

I have lived for thirty-five years in one of the worst climates of the world—India, a land poverty-stricken and disease ridden, "the white man's grave." And yet I have come out of it at the end of these years with a better body than I had when I went in. I have missed only about two single engagements in twenty-five years. (**Abundant Living**, p. 170)

How tremendous is the healing power of the Christian Religion! The Christian Religion inspires healthy living, and this is the best prevention of disease. The Christian Faith, through the creation and sustenance of proper mental, emotional and spiritual attitudes, aids healing through physical methods. Sometimes faith healing and medical science join hands to effect physical healing. Likewise, the Christian Religion is adequate to heal those functional illnesses that have been caused by wrong mental, emotional and spiritual attitudes. And, finally, there are times when physical healing is effected directly by the divine activity apart from any intermediary psychological or physical methods.

In view of all this, what should the church do? The issue seems to me to be well-defined: is the original commission of Jesus Christ to the church to engage in a healing ministry binding upon the contemporary church?

In general, there are three main answers to this question. First, there are those who say that the church as an institution should have nothing at all to do in the field of physical and psychological healing.

They say that the work of the church is spiritual; and that the work of healing is outside the spiritual realm. They contend that while the church's work consists wholly in the healing of the soul, the healing of the mind belongs to psychiatry, and the healing of the body to medicine and surgery. Those who hold this viewpoint believe that the church should mind its own "spiritual" business and not meddle with the business of medical science.

Quite indicative of this attitude are the pronouncements of a prominent minister, the mention of whose name will serve no worthy purpose, who has assumed the role of a Modern Defender of the Faith and who styles himself the rightful leader of true evangelicalism. In a sermon on the strange topic, "Divine Healing—Is It A Sign of the Apostasy? What should Christians do about Healing?", he made the following startling statements:

Faith healing is one sign of the apostasy.

The elders spoken of in the Epistle of James were trained men who had knowledge of healing oils. They both prayed and doctored.

Divine healing is as absurd as divine bed-making, divine potato peeling, divine orange squeezing.

Faith healing is just another of Satan's schemes to kill men before they can accept Christ.

Faith healing is a doctrine of the devil.

I reject this first mentioned attitude concerning the relation of the church to a ministry of healing as un-Scriptural, un-Christian and un-historical.

A second attitude toward the church and healing is that evidenced by those who believe that the church should take the place of all other healing agencies. These people believe in ignoring medicine, medical aids, surgery, psycho-therapeutic aids, hospitals, doctors, surgeons, psychiatrists—they refuse to have anything at all to do with any non-spiritual means of healing. They believe that all healing should come through the spiritual power which is entrusted to the church. To them the worship service of the church becomes the medical and psychological clinic. The church becomes the hospital and dispensary. The minister becomes the intern, the physician, the surgeon, the psychiatrist. Spiritual devotion and discipline become pills and anti-septics and treatments. And these folks believe that to seek healing outside of the spiritual power of the Christian religion, to seek it through physical and psychological methods, is definitely a lack of spiritual faith and a distrust of the power of the Almighty.

I reject this second-mentioned attitude as unrealistic, illogical and utterly impractical.

There is the third attitude concerning what the church should do in respect to healing, and this to me is valid and vital and worthy: the Church of Jesus Christ should proclaim the Gospel of Health and of Healing; it should point those who come under its influence to Him who is the source of healing for the total personality; and it should engage in a continuing ministry of healing.

The performance of an active ministry of healing was a distinct part of the original divine commission to the church. On the basis of those New Testament Scriptures relating to "the gifts of the Spirit" being given "for the good of all" it is logical to assume that whenever the gift of healing is manifest, it is through the church as a spiritual fellowship, and not primarily through solitary individuals, however saintly. And, furthermore, there can be discovered no Scriptural nor post-apostolic evidence that the Divine Command to the church to perform a distinct ministry of healing has ever been annulled.

The late Peter Marshall seemed to have sensed the Divine Command to the church to engage in a healing ministry when in a sermon entitled "Research Unlimited," he declared:

God has not withdrawn any power that was available in the days of the first disciples.

There is certainly no indication in the Bible that the power given to them was for a certain period only, or to work in a certain location. If the other elements in the gospel message were to have universal application, and to hold true until Christ returned, why not this element of healing, that has always had such a strong appeal to human hearts and is so wistfully remembered by those in trouble?

There is nothing in the Gospels to give the slightest hint that Christ ever thought that sickness would in any way help man's spiritual life, or that the kingdom of God would be furthered by bad health rather than by good health.

Everywhere he went, Christ was confronted with sickness and disease, and everywhere he did something about it.

"But," someone will say, "that was all very well for Christ to do these things, for, after all, he was the Son of God. He had powers unique as he himself was unique."

True—but he promised the same powers to his disciples. Christ said: "Verily, verily, I say unto you, he that believeth on me, the works that I do shall he do also; and greater works than these shall he do; because I go unto my Father."

Now for some reason or other, we are inclined to skip over that promise, or to spiritualize it, as though by the passing of the centuries the words have lost the meaning they apparently had to the first disciples.

I propose to discuss briefly under the following five headings what I believe should be the activity of the Christian church in regard to healing: a teaching ministry, a ministry of worship and fellowship, a redemptive ministry, a cooperating ministry, a healing ministry.

1. *The Teaching Ministry of the Church in Relation to Healing.* The church must emphasize the truth that religion and faith and salvation relate to the total personality. The church must teach people about themselves: on the one hand, how the strong, destructive emotions of anger, hostility, fear, anxiety, resentment, frustration help to bring about illness. And, on the other hand, it must teach the healing power of the replacement of these destructive emotions with the positive emotions of confidence, hope, friendliness, affection and love. The church must proclaim the gospel of health. It must teach the principles of healthy living, and declare confidently that Christian living is the best prevention of disease. Likewise, the Christian church must announce anew the relationship of its own distinctive ethic of love to health—that harmonious relationships make for the inner harmony of the human personality; that wrong human relationships in any area help to effect personality disharmony.

2. *The Church's Ministry of Worship and Fellowship in Relation to Healing.* The church should develop continuing opportunities for meaningful spir-

itual worship and for well-rounded Christian fellowship. Personal participation in such spiritual worship and Christian fellowship makes for health. Such spiritual activities, likewise, encourage growth in faith and character, and this in turn has a healing beneficence. The Sacraments are also healing in their influences.

The church in its encouragement of private devotion and prayer can, likewise, carry on a ministry of healing. E. Stanley Jones reminds us of the possibility of "continuous" healing through continuing prayer:

"If we are identified with Jesus in prayer as cooperation, then His very life comes out in our bodies, quickening them, reconstructing them, making weak tissues and nerves into strong tissues and nerves . . . This is healing by His very presence within—His life coming out in our mortal bodies . . . We cultivate His presence, and He in turn permeates us with His health."

(Growing Spiritually, p. 293)

3. *The Redemptive Ministry of the Church in Relation to Healing.* When we speak of the redemptive ministry of the church, we do not refer to any work of redemption on the part of the church *per se.* Rather we think in terms of the church as the institutional channel through which flows the redemptive grace of our Lord and Saviour Jesus Christ. The source of redemption, of salvation, of healing, is Jesus Christ.

The church must continually offer the grace of the Lord Jesus Christ as the only antidote for sin and for all negative and destructive emotions; and it must train people to participate personally in the disci-

plined appropriation of divine grace for daily living.
The church must constantly point those who come
under its influence to Jesus Christ, the great physician,
and train them in the art of the discovery of His total
healing power.

4. *The Cooperating Ministry of the Church in the
Field of Health.* The church must cooperate with every other legitimate agency in the prevention of disease, in the care of the ill, and in the healing of those
who are sick in soul, mind and body. Certainly the
church should work in the field of the prevention of
disease. A former medical missionary in India gives
an apt illustration at this point:

Consider, for example, tuberculosis, one of India's most
dread scourges. Suppose I had been able to cure a tubercu-
lar mother by the laying on of hands. I would rather join in
the warfare against the practice of shutting up young girls
for days before and after childbirth, one of the most frequent sources of the disease. When people say, as occasionally they still do, "I only believe in medical missions," have
they any idea how the medical work could carry on if the
church by evangelical and educational work were not cast-
ing out the devils of superstition and ignorance? "If you do
curative work without an equal measure of preventive work,
you are mopping up a flood on the floor while the tap is still
running," says one of India's medical experts. (**The Methodist Recorder**)

The church must point its people to every possible
source of healing. There must be the closest cooperation between minister and surgeon, between minister
and psychiatrist. The church must inspire and support
a practical healing ministry through its clinics, dis-

pensaries, sanitariums, hospitals, rest homes, and nursing centers.

Likewise, the church must be effective in its ministry to those who are ill and to those in hospitals and mental institutions. The church should aid in securing more adequate facilities for the care and the healing of the sick.

5. *The Church Should Afford Opportunities for Definite Healing.* To me this means two things: the Christian minister must be able to guide his people in taking the healing steps; and the church should conduct healing services.

It is my deep conviction that in the case of organic and structural illnesses, reasonable and normal physical and psychological methods of healing should be employed, first of all. Reputable physicians and surgeons should be consulted and their matured advice followed. Proved medical methods and treatments and medicine should be employed. Christian psychiatrists should be permitted to give their diagnoses and prescribe their remedies. Much organic and structural illness is cured as the result of such physical methods of healing.

But what if reasonable and normal physical and psychological methods of healing are ineffective and fail to heal a person? It is my conviction that such a failure of reasonable and normal physical and psychological methods of healing becomes an opportunity for a person to seek healing through the direct divine activity.

The Christian minister must be able to guide a

person seeking such divine healing through the necessary healing steps. I shall mention six healing steps.

(1.) *Relaxation.* In seeking healing the body must be relaxed and freed of all tension. In fact, the body must be "forgotten" so that the mind can concentrate on God and on His healing power. The mind must also be relaxed. Just as the sky cannot be reflected on troubled waters, so the presence of God cannot be realized by a restless spirit. "Be still and know that I am God" (Psalm 46:10). "In quietness and in confidence shall be your strength" (Isaiah 30:15).

(2.) *Purging*: The sub-conscious mind must be cleansed of all wrong emotions and sinful states, so that the healing power of God can flow through it. There must be the consciousness of divine forgiveness in the soul. God's healing power can work only in those who are living in accord with his laws. "Blessed are the pure in heart: for they shall see God" (Matthew 5:8). A person must rid himself of anything and everything that would keep God from working effectively in his life.

(3.) *Clarification.* A person must be specific, not general, in his request for healing. Visualize exactly your need and your desire. Tell God exactly what you are asking for. Don't be vague. Even go a step forward and visualize yourself as healed in the particular physical area of your need, if your prayer is answered.

(4.) *Anticipation.* As one seeks divine healing, there must be an eager expectancy, the attitude of an active faith. Never must a seeker think in terms of failure. Always there is the anticipation of God fulfilling what he has already promised.

In his discussion of faith and its relation to divine healing in his volume, *An Autobiography of Prayer*, Albert E. Day gives a pertinent and practical analysis of what is really involved in an active faith. Faith is, first of all, the acceptance of a thing as beneficial —for illustration, one's employment of prayer to effect healing. Faith is also the reception of an idea as true —for example, one's belief that healing power is available. Faith is, likewise, the acceptance of a personality as real—to illustrate, the consciousness of your own personality as a psychosomatic reality, subject to spiritual laws as well as physical; and the confidence that God's personality is Master of both the physical and spiritual realms.

Thus faith means absolute fidelity to all these ideas: a fidelity which manifests itself in a certain quality of life—living by prayer, living in quest for and in acceptance of the healing, life-giving power, living as if spiritual laws were as important as physical laws, living as if God were Master in both areas and would demonstrate his mastery if we give him the required cooperation.

But faith for healing is even more—it involves the use of the imagination. It demands that one should sustain in imagination only pictures of God at work in his body: annihilating germs, subduing toxins, repairing diseased tissues. Lightfoot's translation of

Hebrews 11:1 suggests that "faith is that which gives reality to things hoped for."

Dr. Day, also, points out that one of the chief obstacles in healing is the "old mind-set," the preoccupation with disease or some habitual notion about its incurability, or some stubbornness of opinion which once having denied the possibility of spiritual healing, is reluctant to admit its error. He affirms that God is equally helpless before the negatives of intellectual doubt and before negative imaginations.

And so, in seeking healing, there must be the spirit of anticipation.

(5.) *Consecration.* One of the conditions of divine healing is this spiritual attitude of the absolute relinquishment of one's life to the will of God. Such consecration is, likewise, one of the healing steps, and an absolute requisite.

(6.) *Appropriation.* The final healing step is that of appropriation—to receive what God has promised, to begin acting in the strength of the healing power received, to be grateful to God for the reality of the healing power in one's life. "Father, I thank thee," is the consummation of the personal appropriation of the divine blessings.

Not unmindful of the divergence of opinions at this point, I am convinced that the church should conduct public healing services. I believe the public healing services can be carried on in such a fashion, under such auspices, that the result will be both spiritually inspiring and physically beneficial.

Occasionally there may be conducted by the church

a healing mission—a series of healing services on consecutive days. Such an occasional healing mission
has many advantages: it affords an opportunity for
more adequate instruction in healing; it gives more
occasion for the development of a proper spiritual
atmosphere; it permits the local church to utilize the
leadership of an outside person experienced in the
field.

I am thinking, however, primarily of the healing
service conducted by the local church as part of its
regular and continuing ministry. Sometimes this healing service is conducted weekly; sometimes bi-weekly;
sometimes monthly.

The healing service should be open to the public.
Nevertheless, I think that only those individuals seriously interested in the relation between religion and
healing should be urged to be in attendance. The
healing service should be conducted in a place that
is suitable for meditation and devotion, and during
such a service, ample opportunity should be given for
such personal meditation.

A healing service might be conducted in the following sequence:

Period of private meditation and prayer.
Scripture (the reading of one of the healing mira-
cles of Jesus Christ).
Prayer, by the leader.
Testimonies to Healings, by those present.
Meditation, by the leader, on some phases of divine
healing (the field for such meditations is unlimited
—Scripture texts, Scripture incidents, the laws of

health, the principles of healing, contemporary testimonies to healing).

Prayers for definite healings.
Period of intercession.
Benediction.

For the period of prayer for definite healing, those interested in receiving such healing for themselves should be invited to come forward, with bared head, and kneel at an altar rail. Then together the suppliants could pray such a prayer as this: "Lord, I know that Thou canst heal me. Fill me at this moment with Thyself. Let every part of me—body, mind, spirit—be filled with new life, for Thou art life. Cleanse and forgive me of all sin and make me whole. Heal me so that I may be an instrument of love in Thy service. Amen." Then could follow the laying-on of hands by the leader, accompanied by a very brief prayer for healing for each person individually.

After the prayers for personal healings, it would seem wise at most healing services to have a period of intercession, during which those in attendance would be asked to intercede for those persons known to be in need of definite healing.

Such a healing service as this outlined above can be conducted on a high spiritual level; it offers spiritual inspiration to those in attendance; and it results in definite healing blessings and acts.

Permit this closing personal word. I long to see the ministry of healing restored to its rightful place in the Christian church, for I believe that if it were, a mighty spiritual awakening would take place within the life of the church. I just as earnestly desire that Christian ministers become "workmen who need not to be ashamed" in their ministry of healing, for in such a ministry they will fulfill more adequately their calling as "ministers of life."

But let it always be kept in mind that after all, physical healing in itself is not the most important divine gift. Rather, the ultimate aim of healing is always the patient's unity with God, and this has priority over the recovery of his physical health. Of course, it is a miracle to be healed physically and psychologically, but it is a far greater miracle when men and women are healed spiritually. True healing is the entire person made whole — with body, mind and soul redeemed and cleansed and harmonized. Holiness is truly wholeness!

CHAPTER VII

NOT ASHAMED—IN HIS RELATIONSHIP
TO THE WORLD

"I pray not that Thou shouldest take them out of the world, but that Thou shouldest keep them from the evil." (John 17:15). ". . . .be not conformed to this world; but be ye transformed by the renewing of your mind. . " (Romans 12:2.) ... "For here have we no continuing city, but we seek one to come." (Hebrews 13:14.)

The Christian minister involuntarily and inevitably finds himself related to three worlds: (1) the secular world; (2) the world of religion; and (3) the world-to-come. Only as the minister achieves for himself a proper relationship to each of these worlds can he fulfil an effective, spiritual ministry. It is our purpose in this chapter to try to discover how it is possible for a minister to be "not ashamed" in his relationship to the world.

THE WORLD OF RELIGION

We begin by discussing the Christian minister's relationship to the world of religion. Naturally, being a religious leader, the minister is inextricably bound to the world of religion. And the minister must understand thoroughly this world of religion if his ministry is to be contemporarily effective.

The minister finds himself, first of all, a part of a

DENOMINATION. I assert unhesitatingly that a minister ought to be an expert in his understanding of and his ability to interpret the "major concerns" of his particular denomination. Let's take a Methodist minister, for example. He ought to know intimately the story of the origin and the history of Methodism. The Methodist minister should be well informed concerning the distinctive doctrines of Methodism. When asked by a theologian or by a lay person, "What is a Methodist?", he should be able to answer intelligently concerning Methodist doctrine. I suppose that a Methodist minister would list for a theologian the distinctive doctrines of Methodism in terms like these: the universality of the offer of Divine Grace; a personal experience of repentance and faith; Christian perfection; the witness of the Spirit; Christian discipline; social holiness; the ministry of the laity; evangelism.

Or perhaps you would speak of the distinctive doctrines of Methodism to a lay person in language like this: Methodists believe that if you don't have true religion, you know you need it (the doctrine of sin); if you want true religion, you can have it (the doctrine of the universality of salvation); if you have true religion, you know that you have it (the doctrine of the witness of the Spirit); if you do not use your religion, you will lose it (the doctrine of social holiness); if you use your religion, you will find it progressive, adequate, increasingly satisfying and effective (Christian perfection); if you want to keep your religion, you will have to share it (evangelism).

The minister must also know the organizational

structure of his denomination. This would include a general knowledge of the present leadership of the church. Likewise, should the minister know both the present fields of service of his denomination and the opportunities for expanded service which challenge his denomination. And certainly the minister should be adequately acquainted with the immediate spiritual goals set by his denomination and with the detailed programs which have been set up in order to help the denomination attain those objectives.

But the Christian minister has more than a relationship to a denomination; he is, likewise, a part of a glorious EVANGELICAL TRADITION. He is an evangelical minister in the tradition of St. Paul, of Martin Luther, of John Wesley, and of a host of other "greathearts" of the Christian Faith. The Christian minister must understand the genius and the origin of Protestantism. He must know something about the spiritual pilgrimages of its leaders and of its history during these post-Reformation centuries.

The Christian minister must understand thoroughly the mighty spiritual principles of Evangelical Christianity, as re-discovered in the Protestant Reformation, and must be utterly true to them in his ministerial life and preaching and spiritual activity. All of the specific principles of Protestantism resolve themselves into the one general principle of evangelical freedom or freedom in Christ, in contrast with the religious tyranny and spiritual despotism exercised by the Roman Catholic Church.

The specific principles of Evangelical Christianity

are five in number. Protestants believe in the right of
private judgment, as opposed to the doctrine of the
sole right of the Church to interpret spiritual matters.
Protestants believe in the doctrine of justification by
faith alone, as opposed to the superficiality, the ex-
ternalism, and the irrationality of sacramentarianism,
sacerdotalism, and ecclesiasticism. Protestantism affirms the principle of the supreme authority of the
Holy Scriptures, over against ecclesiastical tradition,
on the one hand, and a shallow and barren rationalism,
on the other. A further principle of Protestantism is
the sanctity of the common life, which is sharply
opposed to both the clericalism and monastic ascetism
of Roman Catholicism.   And the fifth principle of
Protestantism may be spoken of as the self-verification
of faith. To the Protestant Christian the Spirit of God
witnesses from within to the reality of his own salvation and religious life, so that he may confidently
affirm: "I know whom I have believed." How far
superior spiritually is such a self-verification of faith
to that which is only a church-verification of personal
faith and which says from the outside to a person:
"You may, or you may not, say that you are saved."

The Protestant minister must also understand the
characteristics and trends of contemporary Protestantism as it embraces throughout the world all the
major evangelical denominations. As I look out over
the world of contemporary Protestantism I am impressed by five spiritual characteristics. First, it would
seem that Protestant theological trends are definitely
away from an extreme liberalism in the direction of a

moderate orthodoxy, or at least a moderate neo-orthodoxy. Professor Harold B. Kuhn stated recently in a theological paper that there is a "swing away from mysticism" in theological circles and a trend towards an "all-out acceptance of historic doctrine." Dr. Kuhn also reported a "stress upon the Evangel rather than upon the social gospel." Said he, "A deep skepticism with regard to all absolutes has crept into our nation. This has served as a solvent for the social gospel. There is again assertion of the unity of the Bible, even among liberals." (Quoted in *The Alliance Weekly*.)

In the second place, I note in contemporary Protestantism encouraging signs of an awakening spiritual life. I am not meaning to suggest that we are as yet experiencing widespread spiritual revival in our day. But the very fact that the major denominations recognize that such widespread spiritual revival is not yet a reality seems to me to be a frank admission of the need for such spiritual revival. Such encouraging signs of an awakening spiritual life on the part of the church include such things as spiritual revivals in isolated locations across our nation and the world; the establishment and growth of spiritual "cell groups"; increasing support of Christian missions; and the adoption of specific denominational programs, such as the new Methodist Quadrennial Emphasis upon the Local Church, which are aimed at the development and nurture of spiritual life in the local church.

A third characteristic of contemporary Protestantism is the increased spiritual activity of laymen. Early Christianity was truly a laymen's movement.

And modern Protestantism is rediscovering the significance of laymen in the carrying forward of its spiritual programs. Everywhere there are signs that dedicated lay folk are no longer content merely to "serve tables"; they are likewise giving themselves to "prayer and to the ministry of the word."

I mention a fourth aspect of contemporary Protestantism. There appears to be a quickening of the conscience of the church in regards to its responsibility for the spiritual well-being of those outside its life and for the Christianizing of all social relationships. I see signs of a reviving interest in Christian evangelism both at home and abroad. And I am confident that in many places "the people called Christians" are becoming acutely concerned about the will of God being done in such social matters as nuclear power, racism, colonialism, war, human freedom, economic injustice, corruption in government, family life, and such social evils as the use of intoxicants and narcotics, and gambling.

And we will never understand contemporary Protestantism unless we know something of the ecumenical trends in its life and activities. There is growing up and taking shape in our world today a very definite Protestant solidarity and strategy. Such an ecumenical trend is an absolute imperative for the church, for we are living in a period of history which is predominantly ecumenical. "One world" demands "one church"— if not "one church" in organization, certainly "one church" in essential doctrine, in spiritual objectives, and in common strategy. Protestantism in its battle

with the world needs a long-range view. To win a
battle involves tactics; but to win a campaign demands
strategy.

At the same time that we find ourselves somewhat
encouraged by an apparent spiritual awakening within
contemporary Protestantism, we must not permit ourselves to be blinded to the realistic fact that our day
is, likewise, witnessing a resurgent Roman Catholicism. President John A. Mackay, of Princeton Theological Seminary, has summarized the evidence of this
contemporary resurgence of Roman Catholicism in the
following five-point analysis. There is an awareness
on the part of Roman Catholic leaders that ground is
being lost, especially in Latin America, Italy and Spain.
And in the United States of America each year there
are more converts from Roman Catholicism to Protestantism than from Protestantism to Roman Catholicism. In the Roman Catholic Church there is a growing
concern about the relevance of Jesus Christ to history
and to the common life. There is also a growing interest
in the Holy Scriptures. For illustration, the Rev. Agos-
tino Bea, S. J., Confessor to Pope Pius XII, recently
asked for a revival of the ancient custom of reading a
portion of the Bible at every Roman Catholic mass until the entire Scriptures are covered during the year.

Likewise, the intellectual movement, known as
Neo-Thomism, with such leaders as Maritain and Gil-
son, is in effect a renascence of medieval Roman
Catholic theology. And finally there is evident in the
Roman Catholic Church a resurgent clericalism. Such
clericalism means the pursuit of power by a religious

hierarchy carried on by secular methods for the purpose of social domination.

And, so, we have discovered the Christian minister as a part of his own denomination and as related to a glorious evangelical tradition. He is, likewise, related to THE WORLD OF RELIGION IN GENERAL. Looking at our world from a religious viewpoint, what are its dominant characteristics? For one thing, our world is not at all Christian, either from the viewpoint of numbers or from that of the quality of the life of society. This fact in itself makes our world a mighty field for Christian evangelism. In our nation alone there are multitudes who need to experience in a personal way the reality of the redeeming grace of Jesus Christ.

In speaking of our world as a tremendous evangelistic opportunity we are confronted by another of the sobering characteristics of our contemporary age. Tragically, the Christian Church has permitted the initiative in world-evangelization to fall into the hands of non-Christians. Throughout our world there are evidences of the resurgence of great ethnic religions, such as Hinduism and Islam and Buddhism. And then when we consider such political movements as nationalism and communism which because of their frenzied zeal and ultimate goals are, in reality, "religions," we discover to our shame how far behind the Christian offensive is lagging. Fifty years ago there were not more than ten known communists in all the world; today the communists control 800 million people.

We are, likewise, living through a period in the

religious history of our world when the work of Christian missions is becoming increasingly difficult. In many lands doors to Christian missionaries have been closed. And in other lands the work of Christian missionaries continues under restrictions and in the presence of staggering difficulties. But a thrilling truth has emerged out of all this—the virility of the indigenous leadership of the Christian Church in non-Christian lands has been discovered, and native Christian churches carry on with amazing spiritual success.

How true it is—the Christian minister is a part of the world of religion—whether that world of religion manifests itself through one's own denomination, or through the great Evangelical Tradition, or the world of religion in its most general and universal aspects.

THE SECULAR WORLD

Naturally the Christian minister is a part of the secular world. It was never intended that we should live apart from the world. Jesus in praying for His followers never prayed that they should be taken out of the world. It is not the purpose of the Christian religion to make it possible for a person to be holy only in a hole.

It is incumbent upon the Christian minister that he understand the characteristics and trends of the secular world to which he is unavoidably related. Generally speaking, what are the characteristics of our contemporary secular society? First of all, we are living in an ecumenical era. The world has become a neighborhood. As far as time and space are concerned it is one world. At the present time no place in the world is more than sixty hours away from any other place. In the new jet age this time will be cut nearly in half.

But this ecumenical era presents a tragic paradox in the life of the world, for we discover a world brought closer together by science and yet split further asunder by ideologies. It is a paradoxical world of cohesion and cleavage, of cooperation and conflict, of divisiveness and interdependence, of resurgent rationalism and international cooperation, of furious re-armament and of passionate talk of peace. Hence, it is a world of contradictions, of awkward choices, of calculated risks, of apparently incomparable situations. In such a world the central problem of the democracy-loving Christians will be to attempt to reconcile these contradictions.

We are, likewise, living in a revolutionary age. In the closing lines of his play, "The Glass Menagerie," Tennessee Williams voices a cry which may be heard from many who can see what is happening in the world today. "Blow your candles out," he says, "for nowadays the world is lit by lightning."

The revolutionary character of our age is seen vividly in its rapidly-changing political pattern. I am thinking particularly of the phenomenal way in which monarchical forms of government have been dissolved and democratic governments have been established. In the last decade six hundred million peoples have tasted sovereign liberty for themselves.

A capsule lesson in the history of monarchy may

be had just by looking at the list of signers of the Constantinople Convention of 1888, recently much in the news as the controlling agreement on the Suez Canal. The convention was signed in the name of: Her Majesty the Queen of the United Kingdom of Great Britain and Ireland, Empress of India; His Majesty the Emperor of Germany, King of Prussia; His Majesty the Emperor of Austria, King of Bohemia, etc., and Apostolic King of Hungary; His Majesty the King of Spain, and in his name the Queen Regent of the Kingdom; The President of the French Republic; His Majesty the King of Italy; His Majesty the King of the Netherlands, Grand Duke of Luxembourg, etc; His Majesty the Emperor of All the Russias; His Majesty the Emperor of the Ottomans.

Of these signers, the President of the French Republic is still in business, but only two of the others are—but one is no longer Empress of India, and the other is no longer Grand Duchess of Luxembourg.

This is truly an era in which the colored masses of earth (by far a majority of the world's population) are rising up to throw off the shackles of an old colonialism and the enslaved peoples of the earth are demanding their God-given right to share in freedom. Today all races, peoples and classes demand a share in power and wealth. Arnold Toynbee speaks of the basis of this world revolution in these words of historical insight:

Perhaps the first thing that we have to understand is that the missiles which are now raining down upon our Western heads from Russia and Asia and Africa, and from parts of Latin America, too, are boomerangs that were once hurled into the blue by our own Western fathers and grandfathers. . .

The world revolution is not just an automatic product of our modern Western machine-age; it is also the spiritual offspring of old and cherished Western ideals. For illustration, communism has been hatched out of an egg that was laid in the Rhineland and was incubated in the reading room of the British Museum; and not only Marx, but Gandhi, Ataturk, and Sun Yat-sen have been inspired by echoes of "the shot heard round the world" that was fired at Concord, Massachusetts, in 1775. (Quoted in **New York Times Magazine**)

Toynbee goes on to say in the same article:

Now that the non-Western majority of mankind has made our Western liberal ideas its own, we ought to welcome their demand of equality and liberty as a partial fulfillment of our mission in the world. But because the hitherto "native" majority of mankind is in such a hurry to be treated as human again, it is demanding freedom and power, in certain instances, before it is fully capable of using them aright.

Hence, the great mission of Christian civilization must never again be aligned with those who would deny or thwart freedom; rather it is to aid those who have obtaned their God-given right of liberty to use it for their own ennoblement and for the service of the other peoples of the earth.

But in the midst of these phenomenal seizures of liberty two grave dangers continue to threaten. The first of these is the innate tendency of government itself, even though set up under the auspices of freedom, to make increasing encroachments on the liberties of its subjects. Free peoples everywhere must be vigilant in regard to keeping their hard-won freedoms. Government must ever remain the servant of its people and never be permitted to become a cruel and despotic master.

The second danger is from without, for free governments continue to be challenged relentlessly by various forms of totalitarianism. Here again the price of freedom is an eternal vigilance. In our day democracy's chief foe, from without, is that political "wolf" in a sheep's economic clothing, which we know as Communism. Because of Communism freedom everywhere in our world is menaced.

The Dark Ones trail us over the world, we who would
  bear the light;
And throwing a long, invisible net, slouch barely out
  of sight.
The Dark Ones tangle us foot and neck, and dashing
  our torches down,
Would cap the toil of ten thousand years with a hot
  and smudging crown.

The Dark Ones trail us over the world, like wolves to
  drive us back
To the cave where ape-men grope and prowl, the lair
  of the snarling pack.
And only with guardians many-eyed, struggling in
  fierce unease,
Can we daunt the Dark Ones on the road that winds
  from the jungle trees.

—Stanley A. Coblentz

(Quoted in *The Christian Century*)

It could well be that the most significant characteristic of our secular society is that it is in possession of nuclear knowledge and has at its disposal atomic power to be used for good or for ill, for the saving or the destruction of the earth. This is the atomic age— the era of the hydrogen bomb—and man now possesses the means of his own annihilation.

The clock on the cover of the *Bulletin of the Atomic Scientists* has been moved to two minutes before midnight, with the invention of the hydrogen bomb. (Midnight is thought of as civilization's moment of doom.) Writes the editor of the Bulletin:

> That we live in imminent danger, that an untoward event tomorrow may trigger a tense world to erupt in flames of atomic or thermonuclear warfare, that there will be "no place to hide" for the great masses of civilized mankind— these are the torturous facts which compel our leaders to spell out for us the tragic nature of the times in which we live. . .
>
> The hands of the clock on the Bulletin's cover now stand at two minutes to midnight. Not to terrify, certainly, but to warn and to awaken, the clock is intended to be symbolic. Wishing will not stop the clock. The Bulletin may be wrong. It may actually be one minute—perhaps seconds—to midnight.

Ours is also an age of such mighty technological advances that the prevailing climate of our times is scientific. Ours is an age of science and we think ourselves utterly dependent upon scientific discoveries. And what is the effect of this prevailing scientific climate upon life and human experience? There is no conflict between theoretical religion and theoretical science. The issue is drastically more practical. Science has not invalidated the logic of faith. Rather, it has created an atmosphere in which faith in the Christian sense is becoming more and more unnatural. Science has not created atheists in our age; rather it has developed secularists. While it is true that science has made religion respectable in our day, at the same time it has made personal Christian faith almost unnecessary. Science focuses attention on proximates instead of on ultimates; it offers its "certainties" over against faith's "speculatives"; it robs the individual of his dignified status; and it steadily gnaws at the core of human dependence, which, after all, is the life-line of religion. Perhaps science per se even though it poses under a friendly guise should be viewed by the Christian as really an imposter, and immediate spiritual steps should be taken to try to transform it into a true friend.

Moreover, our age is witnessing a vicious destruction of values. It has been said that our day is the victim of "the acids of modernity." There is no value in our day which is considered absolute; it is either denied or by-passed in some fashion. The sacredness of human life has been deflated. Two major wars within a half-century have made human life but "cannon fodder." The sacredness of truth has been depressed. In war-time the first casualty is truth, and even after the war the casualty doesn't usually recover fully. And what about the "truthfulness" of much modern advertising?

Furthermore, the sacredness of sex and marriage has been debauched. The pagan view of sex as mere self-gratification has under-cut the Christian concept of the human body as the temple of the Holy Spirit and has tended to negate the Christian view of "whatsoever you do, do all for the glory of God." In many quarters marriage is no longer respected as a sacred institution. During the last quarter of a century the divorce rate has jumped from one divorce out of seven marriages to one divorce out of every four marriages.

Even the sacredness of the church as a Divine institution is now being called into question by many. In view of this utter destruction of values in our contemporary age, one is reminded of the words of Holy Scriptures: "If the foundations be destroyed what shall the righteous do?"

This is, also, an age of increasing delinquency and crime and of institutionalized evils. In the U.S.A. fifteen million sex magazines are printed monthly and are read by teen-agers. One million illegitimate babies are born annually. One million girls have venereal disease. Our nation harbors three times as many criminals as college students. A major crime is committed in America every twenty seconds, and crime is increasing at a faster rate than the population.

During a recent year the American public spent twenty billion dollars on gambling and only seven billion dollars on education. Nearly ten billion dollars were spent annually on alcoholic beverages and only three-and-one-half billion dollars on all religious and welfare activities. In 1956 there were 443,057 establishments in the U.S.A. dispensing alcoholic beverages, which represents a total of 137,608 more bars, cocktail lounges and liquor stores than there were churches, synagogues and temples of all religious groups. There are more barmaids in America than college girls. In 1956 the American Medical Association reported 4,589,000 alcoholics in the nation. Everywhere evil is not only rampant but it is becoming more and more institutionalized.

Strange as it may seem, our age is also an intensely religious era. Someone has said that to be religious means for a person to be devoted to something, to some person, to some idea, which he considers to be an Absolute. In our day there is a passionate devotion to Absolutes. Sometimes the devotion is to a brand of religion; at other times it is directed toward a political ideal, such as nationalism. (Perhaps it would be fair to say that some people's religion consists altogether of Americanism.) At other times the passionate devotion is to a leader, considered messianic; for in a revolutionary time it is easier for people to put faith in a personality than in a mere idea.

But in spite of the fact that we are living in an intensely religious era, it is a despairing age. The dominant moods of contemporary life are fear and despair and meaninglessness. There are tensions between disillusionment and hope, between escapism and realism, between skepticism and credulity. Whole segments of the world's population appear to be merely "existing while waiting for extinction." The American people were credited with washing down 7,000,000 sleeping pills per night less than five years ago. Only two years ago the per night consumption had risen to 13,000,000; now it is rated at 22,000,000 pills between shutting down the television sets and the alarm clock hour the next morning. In this "aspirin age" approximately 42,000,000 aspirin tablets are consumed daily, with Americans in their waking hours swallowing aspirin tablets at an average rate of thirty-three pounds per minute.

Ours is a world sorely afraid, an age uncertain of its own future. We hold in our hands the forces of our own destruction, and we are literally scared to death. The literature of the past three decades has been largely the picture of a world of fear and frustration; peopled by victims of heredity and environment. The words of Goethe seem so contemporary: "Humanity twists and turns like a person on a sick-bed trying to find a comfortable position."

The reason for such despair is to be found largely in the fact that modern man has been "trying to spell God with the wrong blocks." Science has been the means of saving human life but it is not salvation for the human soul. Science with all its marvels is doomed to perish apart from spiritual direction. Science gives us instruments of both good and evil without specifying the ends for which they are to be used. Science supplies us with facts and figures, but it is dumb as to their use. Science is helpless to meet the needs of the human spirit and is totally incapable of providing motivation for right conduct. Science, if left to itself, will destroy those whom it purposes to save. We recall the recent penetrating words of Charles A. Lindbergh:

> I saw the science I worshipped and the aircraft I loved destroying the civilization I expected them to serve, and which I thought as permanent as earth itself. Now I under-

stand that spiritual truth is more essential to a nation than the mortar in its cities' walls. (Quoted in **The Spirit of St. Louis**)

Science needs to heed the words of one of its own contemporary leaders, General David Sarnoff:

"The final test of science is not whether its accomplishments add to our comfort, knowledge and power, but whether it adds to our dignity as men, our sense of truth and beauty. It is a test science cannot pass alone and unaided."

And so modern man despairs and will continue to despair until he discovers in both a personal and collective way that "man does not live by bread alone, but by every word which proceeds out of the mouth of God."

What, then, is the dominant characteristic of our society? It is secularism, which is the inevitable result of an exaggerated materialism. Secularism is based solely on considerations of practical morality, with a view to the physical, social and moral improvement of society. It neither affirms nor denies the theistic premises of religion, and is thus a particular variety of utilitarianism. The "spirit of our age" puts the emphasis upon self rather than upon God; upon things instead of values; upon having instead of being; upon flesh rather than spirit; upon succeeding rather than sharing.

The essence of secularism is the relegation of religion, in the historic sense of that word, to a place of little importance, so far as man's life on earth is concerned. The secularist attitude prevalent in our time

has been characterized in these words by a committee
of the American Council on Education:

> Religion continues to evidence itself in fundamental be-
> liefs, in a mood of reverence, and in specifically religious ob-
> servances. Yet religion has largely lost its significance for
> many areas of human activity. Politics, business and in-
> dustry, and the broad patterns of group behavior are no
> longer responsive to definite religious sanctions, however
> much the forms of religion continue to receive traditional
> respect. This is the expression of secularism in recent his-
> tory, not a denial of religion, but the denial of its relevance
> to the major activities of life.

And so a secularistic attitude causes people to "go
through life doped, so as to be insensitive to life's
tragedy."

The Christian minister must not merely understand
the secularistic mood of our modern life but he must
seize the contemporary opportunity to present the
Gospel of Jesus Christ as the only fulfilment of the
unsatisfied longings of mankind, as the only satis-
faction for the void that has been created in the minds
and souls of men by materialism, as the only solution
to the frightening problems of the modern age.

The contemporary world demands both a thought-
ful and a devoted ministry. Men must know both their
contemporary world and the eternal gospel. As a matter of fact this has always been true. Paul knew both
his age and the gospel. His epistles give clear evidence
that he knew the attitudes, desires, ideals, and sentiments of the people about him. It was said of Chrysostom, mighty fourth-century preacher in Constantinople, that he was "a man of the world and a man of

the Word." In other words, he knew both the character of the world and the contents of the Bible. Wesley was, in part, the mighty man that he was because he knew his age. He was an avid reader of history, philosophy, science, political philosophy and many other "secular" subjects. The important thing, however, is that Paul, Chrysostom, and Wesley knew more than their own age. They knew also the everlasting gospel.

The Christian minister must present the faith of our fathers as the only answer for the hysteria of today. The transforming grace of Jesus Christ is the only power adequate for re-making men in an age that has given most of its attention to the manufacture of machines. In Jesus Christ is to be found the only Way, the only Truth, the only Life. The Hon. Ernest C. Manning, statesman of Canada, reminds us:

> We have reached an hour in the history of civilization which I believe is one of the most crucial mankind has ever been called upon to face. We are living in an age in which we see the accumulative consequence of the defects inherent in human nature coming to their climax. I am convinced that the solution is to be found in the application of true Christianity to the lives of individuals and nations.

Arnold Toynbee, whom many consider the world's greatest living historian, has spoken prophetically ominous words: "Our civilization has only a sporting chance to save itself; and this can only possibly be done if it is willing to make a proper adjustment to God and truth."

And when the Christian Gospel is presented in its purity and power, in most instances we shall find a genuine response, for our contemporary society so secular in philosophy and so sorely afraid in spirit remains incurably hopeful in heart.

But this matter of secularism cannot be dismissed by merely referring to our secular society. The Christian minister must understand that secularistic viewpoints and trends are creeping into the very life of the Christian Church itself. Having recognized and denounced the secularism of our contemporary world in general, the Christian minister's spiritual vision must never be hindered by ecclesiastical "blind spots" which keep him from seeing this threatening monster of secularism at the very door of his own soul and at the very threshold of the Christian Church.

To me, and I am speaking utterly sincerely and out of great conviction, this mood of secularism is prone to manifest itself in three areas in the Christian Church: in the temptation to wrong assumptions on the part of ecclesiastical leadership; in the mistaken ideas of the true life of the local church; and in the minister's distorted perspective of his calling.

On the part of denominational leadership secularism manifests itself in the form of ecclesiasticism. This was the great curse of medieval Christianity. The ecclesiastical institution was placed above Jesus Christ, the Lord of the Church. In Dostoievsky's *The Brothers Karamazov*, the Grand Inquisitor appointed by the Church says to Christ who suddenly appears to him: "And tomorrow I shall burn Thee also."

Such ecclesiasticism equates the church with the Kingdom of God and places the leaders of the church practically on a par with Christ Himself. There develops a sort of "Divine Right" of church leaders, because of which church leaders sometimes appear as those who can think no wrong, speak no wrong, do no wrong. This is the spirit that prompts religious leaders to stoop to all kinds of methods in order to be elected to denominational positions. How tragic is the case of a deposed bishop in Europe who thought the episcopacy of a Christian church a prize so socially and politically glittering that he resorted to the mean and furtive device of poison-pen anonymous letters to defeat the candidacies of his rivals. The spirit of ecclesiasticism on the part of denominational leaders often makes them demand that all who would have a favored place in their intimate circle of church appointees must conform utterly to their wish and will.

We must beware of ecclesiasticism in the church. Jesus warned: "Take heed and beware of the leaven of the Pharisees." (Matthew 16:6.) And our Lord would have us to remember constantly that "in this place is One greater than the temple." (Matthew 12:6.)

In the life of the local congregation secularism manifests itself in the adoption by the church of a worldly perspective of what it is supposed to do, and of a worldly set of standards for the evaluation of its work and workers. Recently there has appeared a satirical expose of secularism in the modern church, under the title, *Dear Charles,* written by Dr. Wesley Shrader, former pastor of First Baptist Church, Lynchburg, Virginia, and now assistant professor of Pastoral Theology in Yale Divinity School. Undoubtedly Dr. Shrader gives us an exaggerated picture of the truth;

but the truth remains, and it would serve every minister and church well to examine themselves in the light of this volume which has been called "a merciless expose of tinkling cymbalism." Note the following words from a review of the book:

Dear Charles is a collection of twenty-six fictional letters from Astute, a frustrated seminary professor, to the Rev. Charles Prince, an ambitious young pastor, on how to succeed in the ministry. Like Lord Chesterfield, Professor Astute neglects few facets of the successful man. "I want to begin with your appearance," he says. From dieting to dandruff, he recites his litany. "Your underwear should be chosen with care   You will be stopping at hotels with some of your prominent men. While I am on this subject, a word should be said about the care of teeth and underarm perspiration."

Churchgoers, in Astute's theology, exist to be pleased. "Let your church officials know where you stand on the points which they now cherish more highly than religious doctrines." Sermons, warns Astute, should always be comforting, never political, and preferably critical only of those "outside the fold."

A pastor's goal should be to outdo previous pastors. Since "there is no difference between selling insurance and selling religion," there is no excuse for not increasing the church's rolls, even if it means luring people from other denominations. ("Can you imagine the representatives of General Motors suffering any qualms over taking customers away from Studebaker?") In asking for money ("this is primarily what you are concerned with"), the wise pastor will remind his people that "if you trust the Lord and put in ten dollars, you will get twenty in return."

"A Ph.D.," says Astute, "will open more doors and make more of an impression than anything you could possibly possess." But the Rev. Dr. should not take himself too seriously; he would do well to pass up Toynbee's **Study of History** and devote his "selective" reading to denominational periodicals—the Biblical Bugle, the Biblical Trumpet, the Biblical Clarinet, etc.

Astute believes that his denomination alone has the truth and that the ecumenical movement is "the literal incarnation of Satan." He advises against birth control because it cuts down on the church's membership, cautions against discussing the race problem or labor-management relations because they are too controversial. But he does have his unorthodox moments: "I have long held the opinion—privately, of course—that the Sermon on the Mount is the most impractical nonsense I have ever read."

Pastor Prince is such an apt pupil that he is called to become pastor of the large, powerful First Church in Mammonville—"an honor that angels would covet." But almost before he can turn his charm on the new congregation, he is inconsiderately called to the "bright golden shore." "The magnetic smile, which he has perfected across the years, now in death crinkled slightly about his full lips. Though his eyes were closed, he appeared any minute to be ready to raise himself from his new bondage and greet each mourner by name, with a lusty handshake and a resounding slap on the back." (Quoted in **Time Magazine**, Aug. 22, 1955)

The local church must beware of worldliness. It is not to be "conformed to this world," either in its objectives, or moods, or methods, or its standards of judgment, or in the quality of its life. Rather it is to be "transformed by the renewing of its mind" that it may discover for itself and through itself bring to pass in the lives of others "that good and acceptable and perfect will of God."

As far as the individual minister is concerned, I believe that the secularistic mood of our age attacks him at three vulnerable points: (1) in his desire to be a successful minister; (2) in his over-concern for material things; and (3) in his yielding to the ecclesiastical pressures of any denominational leader in the hope of ecclesiastical advancement or office.

Every minister ought to have the desire to be a success and has the right to be successful. But the Christian minister must make sure that he has a Christian definition of success. Remember the words of Jesus Christ:

> Ye know that they which are accounted to rule over the Gentiles exercise lordship over them; and their great ones exercise authority upon them. But so shall it not be among you: but whosoever will be great among you, shall be your minister: and whosoever of you will be the chiefest, shall be servant of all. For even the Son of man came not to be ministered unto, but to minister, and to give His life a ransom for many. (Mark 10:42-45.)

To be a success as a minister does not mean to be popular in the sense that everybody will like you. "Woe unto you when all men shall speak well of you." (Luke 6:26.) "Blessed are you when men exclude you." (Luke 6:22.) "Blessed are they which are persecuted for righteousness sake." (Matthew 5:10.) Nor does being a success as a minister mean preaching that suits everybody. Rather, it means the courageous declaration of the revelation of God as it is in Jesus Christ. The story is told of a painter who was summoned before the Tribunal. There he received the word that one of his paintings had been considered as an invitation to revolt. It was demanded of him that he paint another picture which would annul the first one. The artist answered: "We, the painters, are artists; we have inspiration and we obey it, even though it displeases the mighty."

Nor does a minister to be a success have to do everything that anybody in a community asks him to do. In that book of rich humor—alas, now practically forgotten—Lloyd Douglass' *The Minister's Everyday Life*—he commends the virtue of "scarcity" to the pastor going to a new city. He urges him not to spread himself all over the local zoo, speaking to the Lions, the Eagles, the Elks and the Moose. He suggests that if anyone wants to see and hear the new "curiosity," he should come to the one place where the man is on exhibition, his church.

When asked, "What is ministerial success?" the late Dr. F. W. Robertson answered:

Crowded churches, full aisles, attentive congregations, the approval of the religious world, much impression produced? Elijah thought so, and when he discovered his mistake, and found out that the Carmel applause subsided into hideous stillness, his heart well-nigh broke with disappointment. Ministerial success lies in altered lives, and obedient humble hearts, unseen worth recognized in the judgment day.

The Christian minister must also beware of being over-concerned about material things. Jesus reminded us that we are not to lay up for ourselves treasures upon the earth but we are to lay up treasures in heaven, for where our treasure is there will our heart be also. (Matthew 6:19-21.) Paul in writing to young Timothy told him that "godliness with contentment is great gain"; but that "they that will be rich fall into temptation and a snare." Timothy was exhorted to "flee these things," and "follow after righteousness" and "fight the good fight of faith." (I Timothy 6.)

At a meeting of the Colorado Conference Historical Society, a story was told of a pioneer preacher, who, during the gold rush, had taken a little time off and joined the prospectors in panning for gold. Soon he was giving all his time to the search for gold. Suddenly, realizing his peril, he climbed to a high peak, and opening the handkerchief which contained the gold dust he had washed out so laboriously, he shook it out upon the ground, then held up the cloth that the mountain winds might cleanse it.

Nor must the minister yield to the ecclesiastical pressures of any denominational leaders in the hope for ecclesiastical advancement or office. There are real dangers in worldly offices, and especially when these are in the church. Bishop Jeremy Taylor spoke these words in a former century, but they have contemporary meaning:

Avoid great offices and employments, and the noises of worldly honors. For in those states, many times so many ceremonies and circumstances will seem necessary, as will destroy the sobriety of thy thoughts. If the number of thy servants be fewer, and their observances less, and their reverences less solemn, possibly they will seem less than thy dignity; and if they be so much and so many, it is likely they will be too big for thy spirit. And here be thou very careful, lest thou be abused by a pretence, that thou wouldst use thy great dignity as an opportunity of doing great good. For supposing it might be good for others, yet it is not good for thee; they may have encouragement in noble things from thee, and, by the same instrument, thou mayest thyself be tempted to pride and vanity. And certain it is, God is as much glorified by thy example of humility in a low or temperate condition, as by thy bounty in a great and dangerous. (Quoted in Kepler, **The Fellowship of the Saints**)

The Christian minister must be swift to recognize and resist the encroachments of secularism upon his own life and ministry and upon the program of the local church. "No man that warreth entangleth himself with the affairs of this life." (II Timothy 2:4.) How spiritually tragic when the spirit of the world gets the best of a child of God. "Demas hath forsaken me, having loved this present world." (II Timothy 4:10.)

Every Christian minister would do well to heed continually these words of Samuel Rutherford:

> I see that this world is like a great fire: if a cold man stand at a reasonable distance it warms and comforts him; but if he go into the midst of it it burns him. Men who have an indifferent hold of the world and stand at a proper distance from it are benefited thereby; but those who cast themselves into the midst of it are thereby swallowed up and forever lost. Oh, but poor worldlings get but a paltry heaven!"

In the final analysis the Christian minister's victory over worldliness and "the secular mind" is the result of a personal spiritual experience. The minister must "die out" to his self, to the world, to material things, even to time itself, and live solely for and wholly to God. Oh, that we modern ministers might have that deep spiritual experience of the Apostle Paul: "God forbid that I should glory, save in the cross of our Lord Jesus Christ, by whom the world is crucified unto me, and I unto the world." (Galatians 6:14.) "I am crucified with Christ: nevertheless I live; yet not I, but Christ liveth in me: and the life which I now live in the flesh I live by the faith of the Son

of God, who loved me, and gave Himself for me."
(Galatians 2:20.)

This was the spiritual experience of St. Francis of
Assisi. One of his closest brothers has pictured St.
Francis' death for us, in *The Mirror of Perfection:*

> In the year of our Lord 1227, on the fourth of the nones
> of October, he passed away to the Lord Jesus Christ, whom
> he loved with his whole heart, with his whole mind, his whole
> soul, his whole strength, his most ardent desire, and fullest
> affection, following Him most perfectly, running after Him
> most swiftly, and at the last reaching Him most gloriously.

This was the spiritual experience which prompted
Augustine Baker to declare: "I renounce all care and
solicitude for tomorrow concerning anything belonging
to this life." Such a personal spiritual experience was
the reality behind Isaac Watts' moving lines: "All the
vain things that charm me most I sacrifice them to
His blood."

This is what Emerson meant when he wrote concerning the world: "I can get along without it." And
the Christian minister must mean it too!

THE WORLD-TO-COME

In order to make the picture complete, as we close
this chapter on the minister and his relationship to
the world, we must also see him in his relationship to
the world-to-come. One world is not enough for any
person created in the image of God; and certainly one
world can never be the full measure of any man called
into the Gospel ministry. For after all, in a very real
way, the call to the ministry came to a man from the
Eternal World, as God spoke distinctively to him.

And is it not just as true that the ultimate objective of the minister's labors can be realized fully only in the world-to-come? The minister is concerned primarily with the production of Christian character, and such character will be consummated and manifested fully only in eternity. "Behold, what manner of love the Father hath bestowed upon us, that we should be called the sons of God . . . Beloved, now are we the sons of God, and it doth not yet appear what we shall be: but we know that, when He shall appear, we shall be like Him; for we shall see Him as He is." (I John 3:1, 2.) "And He gave some, apostles; and some, prophets; and some, evangelists; and some, pastors and teachers; for the perfecting of the saints, for the work of the ministry, for the edifying of the body of Christ: till we all come in the unity of the faith, and of the knowledge of the Son of God, unto a perfect man, unto the measure of the stature of the fulness of Christ." (Ephesians 4:11-13.) "Even as Christ also loved the church, and gave Himself for it: that He might sanctify and cleanse it with the washing of water by the word, that He might present it to Himself a glorious church, not having spot, or wrinkle, or any such thing: but that it should be holy and without blemish." (Ephesians 5:25-27.)

The minister's citizenship is in heaven. The minister has "set his affection on things above, not on things on the earth." (Colossians 3:2.) The minister has tasted of "the powers of the world to come." (Hebrews 6:5.) The minister experiences what Francis Thompson describes in these moving lines:

"O world invisible, we view thee,
O world intangible, we touch thee,
O World unknowable, we know thee,
Inapprehensible, we clutch thee!"

The Christian minister feels within himself the mighty forces of a world quite other than the world in which most people seem to be content to live. In Jesus Christ the minister touches the spiritual resources of this Eternal World. It is from this other world into which Christ lifts the minister that he brings that which enables him to meet the demands and bear the burdens of this present world. For this world's tasks the minister finds an unseen strength, for its sorrows secret sources of comfort, for its complexities, light and guidance.

It is the minister's consciousness of the Eternal World that keeps him from losing heart, that saves him from the peril of quitting too soon, that causes him to rise above all discouragements, that makes him faithful to the finish. It was said of Moses that "he had respect unto the recompence of the reward," that "he endured as seeing Him who is invisible." (Hebrews 11:26, 27.)

David Livingstone caught his first glimpse of Victoria Falls a little over a hundred years ago. The sight of that majestic fall of water deep in the heart of the African continent was an exhilarating experience for him. Sense of adventure, sense of mission, ran high in him.

Almost immediately after this—according to his journal—Livingstone came suddenly upon the remains of a Christian church. The signs were almost obliterated, but they were unmistakable. A broken church bell lay half buried in the long grass. There were the remains of an altar slowly breaking up in the stranglehold of tropical growth. It had been a Christian church, founded by the Jesuits long before, and now all memory of it forgotten.

In a mood of dark despair the great missionary halted where he was, with little heart to continue his journey. As his custom was, he made an entry in his journal, setting down his sensitivity to the awful missionary burden, so much to do, and all of it so vulnerable, so soon overthrown. He wrote:

Why should I go on? Is it worthwhile going on trying to open up Africa with its teeming millions to the Christian Gospel when—(and this is one of the few occasions when Livingstone came close to bitterness)—when tomorrow morning I too may be knocked on the head by ignorant savages?

But David Livingstone did go on! And why? He lifted up his eyes away from earth to heaven. He was lured by the Eternal World! In a great personal experience of "seeing Him who is invisible" he realized anew that he should be "steadfast, unmoveable, always abounding in the work of the Lord, forasmuch as ye know that your labor is not in vain in the Lord." (I Corinthians 15:58.)

With what confident assurance the true minister of Jesus Christ approaches the Eternal City as he faithfully pursues his earthly pilgrimage! Paul could declare unhesitatingly to his Philippian friends: "I am in a strait betwixt two, having a desire to depart, and to be with Christ: which is far better; nevertheless to abide in the flesh is more needful for you." "For me to live is Christ, and to die is gain." (Philippians 1:23, 24, 21.)

And he could just as triumphantly write to Timothy, his "son in the faith":

I am now ready to be offered, and the time of my departure is at hand. I have fought a good fight, I have finished my course, I have kept the faith: henceforth there is laid up for me a crown of righteousness, which the Lord, the righteous judge, shall give me at that day: and not to me only, but unto all them also that love His appearing. (II Timothy 4:8.)

The Christian minister is truly a man of the world, for he finds himself in relationship to the world of religion, to secular society, and to the world-to-come. But he must never be ashamed in his relationship to the world. To the world of religion that relationship is one of knowledge and insight; to secular society it is a relationship of transformation and triumph; and for the minister the world-to-come ever shines brightly as the spiritual North Star of consummation and glory!

CONCLUSION

" . . . . I was not disobedient unto the heavenly vision." (Acts 26:19)

A few closing words are in order. The minister must be "a workman that needeth not to be ashamed." His calling is so distinctive, his work is so important, his responsibility is so tremendous. In a very real way the preacher is like the keeper of a lighthouse. Did you ever ponder the sobering responsibility of a keeper of a lighthouse? A spiritual application to preachers can easily be made of these words of Robert T. Coffin about lighthouse keepers.

People who live in lighthouses do a special kind of living. They go up to their work—to whitewash the tower in the Spring, to light the lamp at night   Lighthouse people look up more than we do. There is more to see, and they see more. We look out in one direction. They can see the whole circle of the horizon. Their eyes are keener. They have to be. It is important to them to know the signs of the ocean and the sky, to be able to tell them when the storm is coming . .

The lighthouse men live where they work. That makes a big difference. They keep their houses like their light, polished and shining. They keep their lives the same way. . .

The office is for life, and only taken away through misbehavior. Lighthouse seventy-five feet high: light requires trimming every night.   ." **(Yankee Coast)**

And because of the sobering responsibilities of a minister's calling and life and task, his life ministry is constantly confronted by moral judgment. "Woe is unto me if I preach not the Gospel." (I Corinthians 9:16.) "Every man's work shall be made manifest:

for the day shall declare it, because it shall be revealed by fire: and the fire shall try every man's work of what sort it is." (I Corinthians 3:13.) It was to His own disciples that Jesus spoke such words as these: "And fear not them which kill the body, but are not able to kill the soul: but rather fear Him which is able to destroy both soul and body in hell." (Matthew 10:28.) Paul tells Timothy that the minister must live in the personal consciousness of Divine Judgment: "I charge thee therefore before God and the Lord Jesus Christ *who shall judge* the quick and the dead . . . . preach the word: be instant in season, out of season; reprove, rebuke, exhort with all longsuffering and doctrine." (II Timothy 4:1, 2.)

I must confess that to me the most disconcerting of all the Pauline statements about the Christian ministry is this one: "But I keep under my body, and bring it unto subjection: lest that by any means, when I have preached to others, I myself should be a castaway." (I Corinthians 9:27.)

"I myself should become a castaway"—the word Paul uses for "castaway," according to strict translation, means "disapproved." It is the negative form of the word Paul uses for "approved." How significant to our particular theme—the workman, who because he has not studied to show himself approved unto God, is ashamed and becomes the castaway even when he has preached to others. The approved man hears God's "Well done!" But the disapproved man confronts a silent God and does not deserve a crown of life.

The same word translated "castaway" also appears in Hebrews 6:7, 8: "For the land that hath drunk the rain . . . . and bringeth forth herbs meet for them for whose sake it is tilled, receiveth blessing from God: but if it beareth thorns and thistles, it is rejected (disapproved) and nigh unto a curse." Do you wonder Paul was determined never to become a "castaway?" Almost desperately he cries out, "I run, I fight, I bruise my body, lest I who have been a preacher, I who have sown the good seed in other lives, should at last find my own soul bearing only thorns and thistles, a wasted land, sown thickly with the seed of death."

It's a familiar, oft-repeated story, but so meaningful. An Anglican bishop was instructing a group of ordinands on the eve of their ordination. He said to them: "Young men, tomorrow I will say to you, 'Take thou...take thou...take thou...wilt thou?...wilt thou? . . .wilt thou?' But some day at the Judgment, God will ask you, 'Hast thou?... hast thou?. .hast thou?' "

But the Christian ministry is far more than devotion to duty wrought out in the continual consciousness of Divine Judgment. In response to the Divine Call, under the influence of Divine Grace, in obedience to the Divine Spirit, it becomes a life of thrilling spiritual adventure, of rich and abundant blessing, and of ever-increasing glory. The minister's life becomes the narrative of an eternal personal response to redeeming love. "The love of Christ constrains me."

"Were the whole realm of nature mine,
That were an offering far too small;
Love so amazing, so divine,
Demands my soul, my life, my all."
(Isaac Watts)

"Since from His bounty I receive
Such proofs of love divine,
Had I a thousand hearts to give,
Lord, they should all be Thine."
(Samuel Stennett)

"O for a thousand tongues to sing
My great Redeemer's praise,
The glories of my God and King,
The triumphs of His grace!"
(Charles Wesley)

The minister's life becomes the autobiography of an ambassador to a dream. "I was not disobedient to the heavenly vision." It is a life replete with daily evidences of the sufficiency of God's grace, for what God calls a man to do, He will carry him through. How true it is that "when God orders He gives." In the pocketbook of a missionary who died suddenly at his post in West Africa in 1949 were found these lines:

"Always with more work than we can do, with harder problems than we can solve, with more opposition than we can meet; never seeing how the work is going to be done, and yet when the time comes, doing it—so we do God's work and accomplish His will."

The minister's life is one of unending spiritual adventure, climaxed only in eternity: "I follow after, if that I may apprehend that for which also I am apprehended of Christ Jesus." (Philippians 3:12.) The minister's life is, likewise, one of satisfying memories, and, after all, what is more important as far as human things are concerned? When asked the question, "What sermon would you preach if you knew it were to be your last?" "Dig or Die" Brother Hyde thoughtfully replied:

All right, then, I would want my one sermon to be to young people, maybe along in the middle or late teens. And the sermon would be on memories. I would like to tell them that there are two things in life no person can get away from—himself and his memories. He can run away from home, from school, from a community he doesn't like, from responsibility he doesn't want to accept; in fact, he can escape from almost everything. But a man can never run away from himself or his memories. A store of good memories is the finest treasure a man can lay up on earth, while bad memories make hell out of this present life. "Live so that your memories are good companions to the end of your days." I think that is the one sermon I would preach as my last."
(Dig or Die, Brother Hyde)

The minister's life is one of endless glory. Now it is glory reflected from another world; but then it will be glory consummated in the eternal Presence of God. "The Lord shall deliver me from every evil work, and will preserve me unto His heavenly Kingdom: to whom be glory for ever and ever." (II Timothy 4:18.)

"On Jordan's stormy banks I stand
And cast a wishful eye
To Canaan's fair and happy land,
Where my possessions lie.

"(*Then*) shall I reach that happy place,
And be forever blest,
(*Then*) shall I see my Father's face,
And in His bosom rest."
(Samuel Stennett)

After this I beheld, and, lo, a great multitude, which no man could number, of all nations, and kindreds, and people, and tongues, stood before the throne, and before the Lamb, clothed with white robes, and palms in their hands;

And cried with a loud voice, saying, Salvation to our God which sitteth upon the throne, and unto the Lamb.

And all the angels stood round about the throne and about the elders and the four beasts, and fell before the throne on their faces, and worshipped God,

Saying, Amen: Blessing, and glory, and wisdom, and thanksgiving, and honor, and power, and might, be unto our God for ever and ever. Amen.

And one of the elders answered, saying unto me, What are these which are arrayed in white robes? and whence came they?

And I said unto him, Sir, thou knowest. And he said to me, These are they which came out of great tribulation and have washed their robes, and made them white in the blood of the Lamb.

Therefore are they before the throne of God, and serve Him day and night in His temple: and He that sitteth on the throne shall dwell among them.

They shall hunger no more, neither thirst any more; neither shall the sun light on them, nor any heat.

For the Lamb which is in the midst of the throne shall feed them, and shall lead them into living fountains of waters: and God shall wipe away all tears from their eyes. (Revelation 7:9-17.)

My dear readers, I thank you from the depths of my heart for this privilege of sharing with you through these pages. God help each one of us to be "a workman that needeth not to be ashamed."

the
author

Frank Bateman Stanger, a native of New Jersey, entered the New Jersey Annual Conference of The Methodist Church in 1935, and served pastorates within that Conference for twenty-four years. His most recent pastorate was First Methodist Church, Collingswood, N. J., a church well-known for its evangelistic and missionary emphases.

Dr. Stanger is a graduate of Asbury College, Princeton Theological Seminary, and he earned his Master of Sacred Theology and his Doctor of Sacred Theology degrees at Temple University in Philadelphia.

Dr. Stanger has been a delegate to three World Methodist Conferences, in 1947, 1951, 1956, and was elected a delegate to the General Conference of The Methodist Church in 1956. He is active in Methodist historical circles, serving both as a Jurisdictional president, and as a member of the Executive Committee of the American Association of Methodist Historical Societies.

Dr. Stanger has recently been elected as Executive Vice President of Asbury Theological Seminary, Wilmore, Kentucky.

THIS IS A COMPREHENSIVE and illuminating volume on the work of the pastor in the local church. Dr. Stanger speaks with authority, out of many years experience as an eminently successful pastor. He writes out of his rich educational, evangelistic, and counselling experiences, as a shepherd of souls. Every chapter is rich in the realm of the practical, and lofty in spiritual heights and vision.

Dr. J. C. McPHEETERS
President, Asbury Theological Seminary

DR. FRANK B. STANGER'S new book, "A Workman That Needeth Not to be Ashamed," represents the findings of a minister who also is a pastor. The "Shepherd's Heart" is revealed throughout the volume. Readers of the book, particularly pastors, ····'l find here a great wealth of material which will be of inestimable value in the field of Applied Theology.

Dr. W. D. TURKINGTON
Dean, Asbury Theological Seminary

STANGER is really alive in the pages of this book. It ex-
.. sses the passion of his own creative ministry. The volume is
ᴜₙₐsistently suggestive and well poised. It is particularly so in
·ᵤ discussions of the minister's leadership of the Church, and his
ᵤₒₙsibility for healing leadership in this day of psychosomatic medicine. Dr. Stanger realizes fully the immense significance of these times.

DR. HAROLD PAUL SLOAN
Former Editor,
"Christian Advocate"

IN THESE LECTURES Dr. Stanger has combined the advantage of a varied pastoral experience and a wide observation of the field by diligent study. He has written with clear insight concerning the tasks and opportunities of the present-day minister. The young pastor will find in them a searching call to be at his best for God in every church where he may be called to serve. The more experienced pastor will find them to be a helpful guide in the multiplicity of ministerial activities.

DR. HOWARD F. SHIPPS
Prof. Church History
Asbury Theological Seminary